LESSONS FROM A STREET-WISE PROFESSOR

WHAT YOU WON'T LEARN AT MOST MUSIC SCHOOLS

Ramon Ricker

Lessons from a Street-Wise Professor: What You Won't Learn at Most Music Schools
© 2011, Ramon Ricker

For information about this title or to order other books and/or electronic media, contact the publisher:
Soundown, Inc.
6 Nightingale Woods, Fairport, New York 14450
soundowninc.com
585-223-1885

Printed in the United States of America

Cover and Interior design by: 1106 Design

Publisher's Cataloging-In-Publication Data
(Prepared by The Donohue Group, Inc.)

Ricker, Ramon.
    Lessons from a street-wise professor : what you won't learn at most music schools / Ramon Ricker.

    p. ; cm.

    Includes bibliographical references and index.
    ISBN: 978-0-9828639-0-9

    1. Music trade—Management. 2. Music trade—Vocational guidance. 3. Music—Economic aspects. 4. Musicians—Anecdotes. I. Title.

ML3795 .R53 2011
780/.23   2010912972

CONTENTS

INTRODUCTION
A Little Background

MUSIC EDUCATORS HAVE BEEN doing a fantastic job. The level of musicianship of college-age music majors continues to rise each year. Jazz players are entering as freshmen at skill levels equal to graduate students of years past, and "classical" musicians always seem to raise the bar with their technical prowess. Of course, one can always debate musicianship. Are there really more great musicians today than in the recent past, or are they just more technically proficient? That conversation is for another book, but what I think most musicians, teachers and performers would agree upon is that, on the whole, students entering college today are playing at a very high level and there are more of them than there were 20 to 30 years ago.

Music students get hooked. It's almost like a drug. We want to replicate the successes that come from our own hard work. We are always trying to surpass our personal best. When working on technical passages we keep track of our progress by using a metronome. If we can play a passage perfectly at "quarter note equals 120 beats per minute," we move it up to "quarter equals 124" and so on. When we get something right, we do it again, and again, and again just to see how many times we can play it perfectly. Music is very much like sports in this respect. How many free-throw baskets can I make in a row? How many three-pointers? What's my batting average? How fast can I swim 100 yards? Did I better my last time? Music students are often gifted in academic areas, but the high they get from performing or composing often gives them something that excelling in math does not or cannot give them.

Then there's the thrill one gets from playing a solo, hearing an original composition performed, or playing as a member of an ensemble. Along with striving for one's personal best, a musician is intimately collegial, combining his best with that of others. These unique sources of gratification that music offers has led to increased numbers of individuals who want to devote their lives to music. That translates to more music majors in higher education, which translates to more graduates entering the field as professionals. We certainly have the supply side of the equation covered, but what about demand?

It is difficult to compare apples to apples when collecting music student statistics, but here are some numbers to help put things in perspective. There are more than 1,800 degree-granting music schools, departments and conservatories, and 42,000 music faculty in the U.S. and Canada.[1] The National Association of Schools of Music (NASM) is the accrediting organization for higher-education music schools. It has approximately 625 institutional members, or about one-third of the total number of music programs. Among other things, NASM establishes national standards for music degrees and other credentials. As such, they have statistical information that they gather and share with their members. In the latest information that is available, they report that in the fall semester of 2009 there were 115,147 music majors of all degrees, both undergraduate and graduate, enrolled in U.S. music schools. They also report that the total number of degrees awarded from July 1, 2008 through June 30, 2009, was 21,404.[2] But remember, these are figures from only the 625 schools on the member books of NASM. According to the College Music Society, a much more inclusive organization, there were 326,975 students enrolled in music programs in 2007 to 2008.[3] These statistics include all majors and all degrees. They run the gamut of musical interests to include a music industry major at a two-year community college to an Ivy League PhD musicology student. But, no matter how you look at it, there are a lot of mouths to feed. Let's look at a small sub-set of that 326,975—orchestra musicians.

In any given year there are only about 150 orchestra jobs (on all instruments) that open up in the top 50 orchestras in the U.S.! Unlike many occupations in which people change jobs every two to three years, orchestra musicians tend to stay in a position for a long time. I teach a class at Eastman—*Entrepreneurial Thinking*. And when I talk about orchestral job opportunities, I often start by going through the wind section of the Rochester Philharmonic, an orchestra in which I have played for 39 years. I give the number of different players (not counting subs or temporary replacements) who have occupied each position during that time period.

Flute 1	4	Clarinet 1	2
Flute 2	2	Clarinet 2	2
Flute 3/picc	2	Clarinet 3/bass	1
Oboe 1	4	Bassoon 1	1
Oboe 2	2	Bassoon 2	2
Oboe 3	4	Bassoon 3	1

I apologize if the message you are getting thus far is negative and a little demoralizing, but it's really not that bad. Based on the high level of talent, dedication and drive that I have witnessed as an Eastman School of Music professor, I'm actually optimistic for the profession. If you go into music with your eyes wide open, realizing that it will take more than just stellar playing for you to have a comfortable and fulfilling life, you will not be disappointed in your career choice. The same sense of gratification that "hooked" you in the first place will continue to do so year after year.

Music has always been a field where individuals create their careers. In the vernacular of the 1970s we would say, "Make your own scene." We also used to say, "Where can you do your own thing, and get paid for it too?" That was 40 years ago. Those two statements sound dated today, but they still hold true. The bottom line is this: to be a successful music professional today you have to be pro-active. Don't waste time waiting for something to come to you. The supply side of the equation is definitely covered—you're part of it. It's the demand side that we have to work on. Make something happen. In other words—be entrepreneurial.

> **Lesson:**
>
> Success in music requires more than just fantastic technique and artistry.

What is an entrepreneurial mindset? What is needed to achieve it? This book is about street-level tactics and mindsets. It's a practical and pragmatic guide. It's also about personal experience, and for that reason it's slightly autobiographical. But it has to be to some extent, because the lessons in this book are from real life—my real life—often taken from specific incidents or events. Let's call these examples mini case-studies to learn from. This book offers tips and suggestions that hopefully will help smooth your transition from student to professional, or if you are already in the professional world it may offer you important reminders—important information that is not taught at most music schools. Information that hopefully will allow you to be better prepared as you move into the profession. So, let's get on with it.

CHAPTER 1

Legos and Putting Them Together

Legos

LEGOS. YOU KNOW WHAT THEY ARE, little interlocking pieces of plastic that can be combined in an infinite number of ways. With Legos you can make things like buildings or vehicles. If you don't like what you make, you can continually try to improve it by rearranging the pieces; or you can take your creation apart and construct something else. In music and in life, the knowledge and skills, both musical and non-musical, which you have acquired thus far are like Legos. You put them together to create and build a career. You build "you."

Lesson:

Your musical legos can be combined to construct many different careers.

Of course there are many musicians whose Lego kit is almost a duplicate of yours. Remember those music student statistics from a page or two ago. Your job is to find some pieces that are unique and special. And just as your first attempt at constructing something with Legos may be insipid, oddly shaped and not very creative, your first attempt with your music career may be similar. You may find that you are missing some blocks, but through self-study or with a mentor or a teacher you will be able to find what you need.

1

The point is that if you have musical talent, and if you have worked hard to develop it, you have the building blocks necessary to create a career. The first step is to be musically and technically solid on your instrument. You have to play! Add to that some entrepreneurial savvy and as Dr. Seuss would say, "You'll be on your way!" Remember, your job is to build "You."

You, Inc.

We know that a musician is a person who performs, composes or studies music. An amateur does it for recreation and fun. A professional may do that too, but the difference is this: professionals are paid for what they do. (When I speak about professional musicians I am not just talking about performers. I include composers, teachers and academics in the mix.) Professionals are, in effect, a small business, offering goods and services just as any small business would. Imagine a newly-minted clarinetist from a top music school. She may be a fine player, but what does that clarinetist really offer the marketplace? Who will pay for what she can do? Importantly, for the clarinetist, will it provide enough money on which to live?

Our clarinetist's product is playing music on the clarinet, but what style of music—orchestra, chamber, klezmer, Dixieland, jazz? If the only product she can offer is soprano clarinet (B-flat and A) and she only plays the classical and orchestral repertoire, she better be the best in the world, or at least on the way to becoming the best in the world. This type of musician is equivalent to a boutique store—offering very high quality goods but with limited selections and sharply focused on one thing. Over time, to remain relevant, our clarinetist must expand by continually adding to her repertoire—putting more clarinet product on the shelves. This keeps her challenged and familiar with recently composed music. And just as Chevrolet comes out with a new model of the same vehicle each year, our clarinetist needs to keep her core product in top shape and continually improving as she revisits previously performed pieces, making them better and better. If she wants to diversify and offer more products, she might add the smaller E-flat clarinet or the larger bass clarinet. This creates more possible income channels for her. But as she adds these product lines the quality must be kept at an undisputably high level. She has to really command these instruments and not just dabble in them.

Let's say our clarinetist has added these other instruments to her product line and things are going well. She's getting some work playing chamber music and is getting some calls to sub in the local orchestra. How could she expand her store? That depends on her background and interests. Maybe she plays in a woodwind trio or quintet. If she has a talent for and interest in composing and arranging, she could write for her ensemble. If the music is well received there may be a publishing avenue for her to follow. If she is handy and dexterous she may do some minor instrument repair work. But

> **Lesson:**
>
> Commit to quality. Add more product lines, but expand slowly. Don't dilute your core business.

whatever additional products she pursues to make herself more attractive to the buying public, it is crucial for her to maintain the high quality of product that she is becoming known for.

So you see, building a career as a professional is like stocking a store with products. None of us wants a dingy, musty store that just sells beer and cigarettes. We want our store to sparkle, to exude quality and to be a place where the customer can get the finest there is. As our clarinetist stocks her store, she begins to establish a reputation. Marketing people say she is creating a brand.

What Do You Consider Success?

This is an important question to ask yourself. In a perfect world in which your every dream was realized, and you were successful at everything you attempted, what would that look like for you? Would you be a soloist with major orchestras and perform around the world? Would you be a top singer at the Met or a famous jazz artist with your own group? Would you like to be a celebrity—someone like Paris Hilton, whose job is just being Paris Hilton? Does success to you mean being "famous" or "rich," or are you more altruistic? Maybe you want to "make a difference," and perhaps teach music to under-privileged children or set up a music school in your community. Is music even a consideration when you think of being successful in life? It could be that success to you is finding a partner, a soul-mate with whom you can spend your life. That could be your definition of ultimate success.

"Being successful" is probably different for all of us. If you equate success with "being famous," and you are 45 years old, and don't have management or any prospects of that, have never won a competition on your instrument and have only been a soloist with community orchestras, are you a failure? If success to you means "being famous," then the answer is probably yes. But what about the little wins along the way? I would argue that if you set yourself up to be famous or to have a principal position in a Big-5 orchestra, your chances of success are not very good. So what do you do if you never attain this lofty goal? Do you mope around and think of yourself as a loser? If you "fall back" (a term that I hate) on teaching, for example, are you settling for something less than the best? (People who fall back on anything rarely do as good a job as the person who is doing it as a first choice. There are too many excellent musicians out there who aren't falling back on what they do and are totally into it.)

> **Lesson:**
>
> Think of "success" in small units. Celebrate your day-to-day successes.

I like to think of success in smaller units. When I'm playing second clarinet, if I can make the first clarinetist feel good about what we are doing together, I'm successful. If I can give a good lesson to a student and have him leave my studio ready to dig deeper into what we talked about, I'm successful. If I can add some horn or string parts to a car commercial that lifts up the 30-second spot, I'm successful. These little successes build on themselves. Of course, you should have a dream—something that you aspire to achieve, but don't forget to celebrate the little day-to-day successes.

CHAPTER 2

The Musician's Business Challenge

Let's put on a businessman's hat for a minute and look at a young musician's career from that perspective. What are the challenges facing this person as he or she steps into the profession? One might say a musician's challenge is to utilize and evolve the skills obtained in school in order to excel in a highly competitive market. His or her goals will be to become financially stable and to remain relevant. Here are some possible barriers he or she may face:

- It's a commodity market.
- There is changing demand.
- There are price pressures.
- Reduced resources.
- A highly competitive and large talent pool.

Looking at the barriers can make the future seem pretty grim, but as we progress through this book we'll see that it isn't that bad after all.

It's a Commodity Market

A commodity is a good or a service that is basically the same regardless of who produces it. Oil is oil. Rice is rice. Gasoline is gasoline and chickens are chickens. There is little differentiation between producers,

5

and the price within a region will be about the same. A classic case of a producer who was able to break from the commodity pack was Frank Perdue former CEO of Perdue Farms. Through extensive and brilliant advertising and using a marigold-laden feed that imparted a yellow color to the skin of his chickens, he was able to convince the American consumer that his product was superior to others, and his birds were sold at a premium price.[4]

Perdue was able to rise above the others because he demonstrated, at least in people's minds, that his sunny-skinned chickens were superior. Musicians must do the same thing because, in reality, we operate in a commodity market. Each type of service that a musician performs has a price on it that is either mandated by the musician's union (minimum scale wages) or (if it is non-union) by local custom. The musicians who play wedding receptions or bar mitzvahs in Des Moines, Denver, Las Vegas, Atlanta, you name the city, will expect to be paid in a range that is unique to the area. There will occasionally be a gig that pays considerably above the norm, but by and large there won't be much variation in wages.

Below are some union scale wages for playing a show in four different cities in New York State. The three upstate cities are geographically close in proximity, which is exactly what their scales reflect. New York City, which is widely considered a market unto itself, is considerably above the others.

Rochester	$111
Buffalo	$115
Syracuse	$100
New York City	$187.59

When a contractor puts together musicians for an event, regardless of the geographic region, he could hire the concertmaster of the local symphony or a high school student. Either way the pay for a violinist will be the same. That's a commodity. The market as a whole determines the price for the goods or service. The musicians' challenge is to differentiate themselves like Frank Perdue did, and create a reputation (read: brand) that because of its unique qualities will command a premium price over the others. They can do this by becoming the in-demand player that everyone wants. The person hiring such a person knows that he will get a certain level of performance that is above the norm and is well worth the extra money. When the pay is less flexible, as in the case of a show, a first-call musician might benefit over others by getting literally all the work.

Lesson:

Your challenge is to break from the pack and be noticed.

During the Vietnam War, I was a musician and stationed at the U.S. Military Academy at West Point. At that time we had more personnel on each instrument than was needed to adequately staff any event that had to be played. This surplus of musicians on each instrument meant that for any given service there were always some musicians who were not playing and enjoyed some "off" time. An interesting commodity market was created among the musicians, as we bought and sold our duties. Let's say that I was assigned to play a parade on Friday afternoon. If, for some reason, I wanted to do something else, I would look at the roster, see who was off and ask that person if he wanted to play in my place. There was no negotiating. The price was fixed. Parades went for five dollars and funerals for two. (Funerals were much shorter.) KP (kitchen police—working in the kitchen—it wasn't fun) went for $25.

Looking back, it is evident to me that we created a very efficient market where everyone benefited. The entire West Point band operation was housed in one building, and the majority of the musicians who were single lived right in the building. The married personnel received a subsidy for the number of dependents that they had, and they lived either in Army-supplied housing or off post in one of the neighboring small towns. Because the bachelors (there were no women in the band at that time) lived in the same building as the rehearsal room, it was no problem for them to be ready to play a service on short notice. The married men, on the other hand, had wives who often had jobs outside of the home. This gave them discretionary income. Consequently, it was usually the married guys selling their duty to the single guys. Everyone won. I understand that this buying and selling of duty is not so widespread nowadays. It's a leaner Army.

There Is Changing Demand

Ask any musician who is ten years older than you how business is, and he will probably say, "It's okay, but it was much better ten years ago." If that same person asks the identical question to another musician ten years older than he is, he will probably get the same answer. "It's okay, but it was much better ten years ago." Why was it always better ten years ago than it is today? A possible answer is that the music business constantly evolves, and the person who was busier a decade ago may not have moved ahead with it. Perhaps this person has skills that were well suited for yesterday's business, but not for today's.

In my lifetime alone I've witnessed several major changes in the music business. In the 1970s and '80s our Eastman graduates who wanted jazz careers often did their "graduate school" in the bands of Buddy Rich, Count Basie, Woody Herman and Maynard Ferguson. At the same time symphony orchestras were finding increased support from foundations. They expanded their seasons. They were growing. In New York City, Broadway was a convenient thing to fall back on, but the *crème de la crème* was freelance recording. That is, until synthesizers and samplers appeared on the scene.

> **Lesson:**
>
> Build your career around your talents, abilities and interests.

Synthesizers changed everything in the music industry and made it possible to have a very high-end product, at least to the undiscerning listener. Those musicians who embraced technology and moved with it could hope to remain relevant, but those who continued to do what they had always done probably woke up one day to find that time had passed them by. The industry had evolved without them.

For musicians today, more than ever, it is Generation Entrepreneur or Gen-E. Musicians must put together careers that have several different income streams. One source of income usually doesn't do it all. The good news is that with a diversified set of talents (read: Legos) it is possible to build a career that perfectly suits your interests and strengths. Not only will that help to assure your continued relevance in the business, it will also provide you with a very satisfying and fulfilling musical life.

There Are Price Pressures

There will always be someone who is willing to do something more cheaply than you. Students are typically in this category. Look at the music scene around any music school. Students will be playing for their dinner, or coffee if it's a coffee house or for the door (the number of people who show up and pay the cover charge). Musicians are eager to play; they love to play "their music." Believe it or not, this turns out to be their curse. They give it away too easily. Take jazz musicians as an example. If the gig includes players and music that they really like, they are willing to play for practically nothing. Even in large metropolitan areas musicians will drive miles, hassle with finding a parking place and play all evening and into the night for practically nothing. The upside is that they are networking, staying in the scene, keeping their contacts going and communing with their friends.

> **Lesson:**
>
> Put a fair price on your talent. Don't give it away. Charge what you are worth.

Orchestra musicians do a similar thing. They will usually go out of their way to play chamber music. In this more intimate genre where they can be heard, they aren't as anonymous as in an orchestra. The collaborative effort gratifies them and they have more control over the end product. But chamber music gigs usually don't pay as much as orchestra services. The same person in an orchestra rehearsal who watches the clock, and when the big hand gets to quitting time has his instrument packed up and in his car, will have no problem doing multiple rehearsals for a chamber music concert that will pay what one orchestra rehearsal pays! The unwritten rule seems to be, "Don't worry about money if you love the music, but try to get as much as you can if it's a drag."

Reduced Resources

We read about orchestra financial pressures all the time. Musicians demand a decent wage and when communities and boards have difficulty supporting them, an impasse results. As of this writing, of the 51 ICSOM orchestras[5] (largest in terms of length of season and budget), there are ten with minimum salaries over $100,000. Not surprisingly these orchestras are in large metropolitan cities like New York, Boston, Chicago and Philadelphia, and they all have 52-week seasons. As commonplace as this might seem to patrons in these cities, 52-week seasons are relatively new in the orchestra world. "It was only in the mid-1960s, when the New York Philharmonic became the first orchestra to institute a 52-week season."[6]

With large sums of money infused into orchestras from private foundations such as Ford, Rockefeller and Mellon; and from government sources like the National Endowment for the Arts, the period from the mid-1960s through the 1980s saw astonishing growth and support for orchestras. Even mid-size cities like Rochester, NY, moved toward a 52-week season. Fueled by highly qualified music school graduates, the quality and level of orchestras in cities even smaller than Rochester was raised. Such unparalleled growth proved to be too ambitious, and ultimately unsustainable. From a peak in the mid-1980s until today, contraction in season length, rather than expansion has been the norm for many orchestras. On a personal level, one of my good friends who had played in an orchestra for 45 years turned 65 and went to the Social Security office to apply for benefits. The case-worker looked over his life-long contributions and said, "You made more money in 1990 than you did this year." Sad, but true.

> **Prediction:**
>
> If you decide to play in an orchestra, it will be just one of several income streams for you.

William Cahn, a member of the percussion group Nexus and the former principal percussionist of the Rochester Philharmonic has expressed it well.

> Actually, I was the Chair of the negotiating committee for the 4-year contract that culminated in a 52-week season in 1986/87. We all knew it was an ambitious goal, but to everyone's credit the commitment was made anyway. 1986/87 was perhaps the peak year for the incredible post-war growth of orchestras in middle America. Since that year new forces have arisen to put enormous pressure on the resources of time and money needed to sustain such a high level of support for orchestras, especially in middle-American communities:
>
> - a drastic reduction of classical music exposure in music education, not only for children, but especially in the education of music teachers
> - competition from other arts organizations
> - growth of the Internet
> - consolidation of the music industry (SONY, PHILIPS, etc.) in North America and their focus on mass-market music
> - death of classical music radio broadcasting in North America
> - death of the major Compact Disc distributors (Tower Records, others) in North America
>
> As a result, even though statistics gathered by the League of American Orchestras clearly show that attendance at orchestra concerts has steadily increased since WWII (not decreased, as is so often **wrongly** reported), the problem is that costs have risen at a higher rate than attendance growth. This has placed financial pressures on middle-American orchestras that have resulted in a gradual retreat to sustainable budgets and

an ever-increasing trend to "Musi-tainment" programming, in order to appeal to a larger portion of the public.[7]

As stated earlier, technology has changed everything on the non-classical side of the music business. Synthesizers have found their way into practically every genre from Broadway shows to the one-man band playing tunes with play-along tracks at the local restaurant. Forward-thinking musicians have recognized that synthesizers and samplers are not just a passing fancy. Take drum-set players vs. drum machines. An enterprising percussionist would realize that just because a machine can sound acoustic doesn't mean that every person who buys one can make it sound believable. It still has to be programmed! And guess who is most familiar with what a drum set should sound like? You guessed it—percussionists. If you can't beat 'em, join 'em.

> **Lesson:**
>
> Don't be intimidated by technology. Embrace it.

A Highly Competitive and Large Talent Pool

Okay, so we all agree that it's tough out there. Nobody argues with that, but we don't let it get in our way. Successful people in music are drawn to the music itself. It may sound corny but music and performance can be very addictive. The music profession calls us, and music educators have been doing a great job of getting us prepared. With 40 years of listening to entrance auditions for the Eastman School behind me, I can tell you that the musicianship and skill level of entering college freshmen rises each year.

> **Lesson:**
>
> Entrepreneurial thinking can give you a competitive advantage.

All of this means one simple thing: the market is saturated with many highly-qualified musicians. As a result, basic laws of economics have driven down the market value of the services of most musicians. Remember the musician-as-commodity discussion a few pages ago? As previously said, there is plenty of supply. What we need to do is increase demand, and to somehow find a way to break from the pack.

One way an individual can create a competitive advantage in music is to take charge and make a career. Be pro-active and don't wait for something to come to you. Go after it. Recognize opportunities and don't be afraid to take calculated risks. In other words, be entrepreneurial.

CHAPTER 3

What Is Entrepreneurship and Why Should We Care?

YOU HAVE PROBABLY NOTICED that the word "entrepreneur" is seen in print and heard in conversations more and more lately. I just Googled it (that word seems to be a verb now-a-days) and found nearly 39 million entries. And as I quickly scanned the first three or four pages, I observed that each entry talked mostly about starting a business. So what does the subject of entrepreneurship, being entrepreneurial or being an entrepreneur, have to do with us? We're musicians. We're artists. We play music because we love it. That's true, but we also like to eat and to sleep in a bed at night.

The truth is that musicians, in general, are very entrepreneurial. We have to be, because very few of us can rely on just one type of activity to put enough bread on the table. We may play in an orchestra, but we also might teach at home or at a local school or university. We may repair, refurbish or even make instruments. Some of us play freelance gigs, or compose, arrange and publish music. And others may have "day gigs"

> **Lesson:**
>
> Build your career around "you."

(read: side businesses) outside of music as tax preparers or realtors—you name it. As musicians we usually put together several income streams to create our careers. The good news is that by doing this we craft a career around our strengths and interests—something that is unique to us. Here are some observations.

Be Prepared for a Career That Must Evolve

Now that I'm in my sixties I have the advantage of being able to look back and see how my own career has made certain turns—all for the better I might add. But when I graduated from college I had no idea that someday I would be teaching at a prestigious music school like Eastman or playing in a respected orchestra like the Rochester Philharmonic. We all must evolve with opportunities that present themselves to us and adapt to challenges that face us. Change is good. Learn to embrace it. It keeps us interested and non-complacent. It's impossible for us to know what "the next big thing" will be, but if we have a solid musical foundation and a healthy dose of curiosity, we will be able to take that step into something that may not be so immediately comfortable or familiar. Just as music itself is constantly changing and evolving, the business side of music does so, too. In both cases, musicians must adapt or become irrelevant.

Lesson:

Adapt, be flexible, and accept change. It is inevitable. Don't fight it.

Breadth/Depth

Relevance, regardless of your profession, depends heavily upon the expertise you command. For a musician, if you have a broad knowledge of music, are comfortable playing in a wide variety of styles and know something about music history and theory, you'll have the breadth. Now comes the depth part. You have to have expertise and high proficiency in the areas of your concentration. You have to be competitive with others who are doing the same kind of work that you do. In down-to-earth terms,

Lesson:

Be a life-long student. Continue to expand your musical breadth and depth.

you have to be unbelievably good at what you do. Importantly, as your career develops and the years pass, it's critical that you keep expanding in both your musical breadth and depth. Be a life-long student, and the chances of keeping your edge—ergo, your relevance—increase tenfold.

Musicians Are Already Owners

Corporations spend lots of time and money trying to get their employees to feel like they are stakeholders in their company. If you've ever been a "leader" or the person "in charge," you know what this feeling is like. You feel responsible for the success or failure of a project that is under your supervision. The other hired persons may not care at all—"Just give me the check," they mutter. In contrast, musicians, in general, almost always feel like stakeholders. We are part of, and responsible for, the overall experience. Our playing and reputation is on the line with each performance, and we don't want to let the rest of the group down by screwing something up. We always want to do our best—that is, when it's about the music. But in an orchestra, it's often about non-musical things, to which we often adopt a different attitude. "I just play my instrument. Let management handle that other non-music stuff." There is some justification for this attitude because we haven't been trained as marketers or fund-raisers. However, it is undeniable that when musicians feel that they are part of a team, good things can happen. And it may be as simple as smiling at the audience as we take a bow.

> **Lesson:**
>
> Be involved. Have a stakeholder attitude in all that you do.

It's a Commodity Market (a reprise)

It's worth repeating. By and large musicians operate in a commodity market—something that is more or less the same price in a geographic area. You can drive all over your community looking for cheap gas, but it will be within a couple of cents per gallon at most places. It's the same with milk or eggs. They are virtually the same price no matter what grocery store you go to in your town. In a musical context, if you are called to play in the backup band for a traveling musical act like Josh Groban (just to give an example), the payment will most likely be "scale." That's the same pay if you are the concertmaster of your local orchestra or a freshman music-school student. Rising above the "musician as commodity" level is a big lesson to learn. And one way to do that is to be entrepreneurial in a way that will help you achieve a competitive advantage.

You, Inc. (another reprise)

This is also worth repeating. View yourself as a small business— a store with a line of products to sell. Build it one product at a time. Commit to quality, grow slowly and hire the best to teach you what you don't know. Diversify, be flexible and know the competition. With some hard work you'll craft a career that is fulfilling and unique to you.

CHAPTER 4

What Are the Characteristics of an Entrepreneurial Musician?

A Definition

LET'S START WITH THE WORD ITSELF—entrepreneur. It has no direct translation in English, but it comes from the French word *entreprendre,* which means to undertake or to attempt. The present-day definition of entrepreneur is a little more detailed than the French word from which it is derived. One could say that **an entrepreneur is a person who recognizes an opportunity, envisions its possibilities and creates an enterprise to take advantage of the situation, usually with considerable initiative and risk.** Entrepreneurs are doers. They make things happen. At the University of Rochester and the Eastman School of Music we adopted the following definition:

> ### *The Entrepreneurial Process is:*
> *The **Transformation** of an **Idea** into an **Enterprise** that creates **Value***

This broader definition takes entrepreneurial activities away from a strict business school definition and more readily includes humanists, educators, artists and musicians. Let's look at some entrepreneurial characteristics.

Successful Entrepreneurial Musicians Need and Usually Have. . .

. . . a Broad Education

An entrepreneur needs information that is often difficult to teach in advance. For example, you don't need to know about copyright law until someone tries to steal your stuff, or know about lawyers until someone tries to sue you. Much of this broad education is gained through the experience of actually "doing" and learning from it. Some would call this wisdom. But whatever you call it, you need to consider every situation you find yourself in to be a possible learning opportunity. Whether it goes your way or somewhere else, take a lesson from it and write it down in your entrepreneurial memory. The successful entrepreneurial musician usually doesn't wait for the next opportunity to learn.

> **Lesson:**
>
> Consider every situation a possible learning opportunity. Learn from experience.

. . . a Strong Belief in Themselves

Entrepreneurs are willing to stretch out of their comfort zones to try what others would avoid. They should know that it is okay to fail, and importantly, **they must not be afraid to fail.** Babe Ruth didn't hit a home run every time he went up to bat. Separate your sense of self from yourself as a musician. We all know persons who wrap their personalities into their playing. **You are not a bad person if you are out of tune on one note!** If you separate yourself from the music, project or business it

> **Lesson:**
>
> Separate your sense of self from your musical self. You're not a bad person if you have a bad performance.

will ensure that if you do fail at something, you won't view it as a life failure. It doesn't detract from your worth as a human being. It is just a part of life. And maybe it's not a failure at all, but rather, a learning experience that adds to your broad education.

. . . an "Anything Is Possible" Spirit

Whether you succeed at something or not depends in large part upon your attitude. This is especially important when the going gets rough, which all of us have experienced from time to time. If you truly believe you have the ability to accomplish what you've set out to do, then keep your sights set and press on. Conversely, if you are not really committed to a project or you begin to doubt yourself, it can be too easy to quit when faced with adversity and failure. If you believe in the importance of what you are doing, and you believe you're the person to do it, you can power through whatever prob-

> **Lesson:**
>
> Have confidence in possibilities; hold tight to the belief that anything is possible.

lems you encounter. Just keep reminding yourself that you can do it! "Anything is possible!" Who knows? Your spirit of possibility may make a difference in ways you could never imagine.

. . . a Commitment to Follow Their Dream

But don't kid yourself. Keep both feet on the ground. Make sure that before you commit yourself to the "impossible dream," you have the qualifications and the deep knowledge and expertise to make your dream come true. (Remember the breadth/depth dis-cussion a few pages back?) For example, let's say you have been trained as a classical pianist. You're twenty-five years old and a good player. For some reason you decide that you want to be a jazz pianist and you begin lessons. In reality the chance of your ever becoming a high level jazz pianist is fairly remote. Those important

> **Lesson:**
>
> Prepare yourself to follow your dream; you'll need deep knowledge and expertise.

early years when students soak up the style have passed you by. If you are exploring this other style of music for personal enrichment, go for it; but be honest with yourself and don't force yourself into an area that won't be a good fit. Entrepreneurs take calculated risks, not foolish ones. And most people fail in areas where they don't know what they don't know.

. . . a "Glass Is Half-Full" Attitude

Entrepreneurs must be positive, because much of what they do involves selling their ideas or themselves to other people. There is no room for the Sad Sack, Deputy Dawg[8] personality here. I was once doing a horn section overdub session (two trumpets, trombone and tenor saxophone). On this particular date I had to go back and forth between the control room and the recording area to listen to the playback on the big speakers, and to talk to the producer and client out of earshot of the musicians. Things were going well and I guess I was pretty animated. Toward the end of the session I returned from the booth and said to the guys, "They like us." One of them replied, "No Ray, they like you." He was probably right. The session went well because I was upbeat, kept things moving and was engaged with the producer and client.

> **Lesson:**
> Project a positive image; entrepreneurs are involved in selling their ideas to others.

. . . a Desire To Be in Charge of Their Lives

> **Lesson:**
> Being in charge of your life carries with it an increased responsibility to succeed.

A common frustration that many people face in their jobs is that they are not in control. They feel that they are at the whim of their boss or their board of directors, and if they don't abide by the party line they could be out on the street. On the other hand, entrepreneurs, by definition, do have a sense of control over their lives. On the surface it would seem that they have more freedom, since they have greater control. And that's true, they do have the freedom to set their hours, to make decisions, etc. But this freedom brings with it an increased responsibility. Entrepreneurs are keenly aware that if they fail it's no one's fault but their own. To avoid failure and reach their goals they generally work their tails off. Earlier in this book I said it's okay to fail, but I neglected to say that failure is not a lot of fun.

. . . Great Drive and Energy

This is a given. Entrepreneurs try to make things happen, and that rarely occurs without the drive and the energy to stay with it. But where does this come from? Maybe it's a personality trait or possibly the desire to please a respected friend, teacher or relative. Perhaps it's from the knowledge that it is possible to reach one's potential if the discipline is there to see a project through to its completion.

But if great drive hasn't been part of your package, how do you get it? Maybe the place to start is with the topics found in this chapter. Look at them again with self-evaluation in mind. Do you have an "anything is possible" spirit and an optimistic attitude? If they can be improved, how would you go about doing that? It's a start anyway.

CHAPTER 5

What Is a Brand and Is Yours a Good One?

IF, FROM EARLIER DISCUSSIONS IN THIS BOOK, you have bought into the idea that musicians are small businesses, it is time to take it a step further. Companies spend a good deal of time and money thinking about, developing and protecting their brands, and there are business professionals who think about this on a daily basis. I happen to be married to one of these professionals. She is currently a consultant with her own practice that focuses on the Arts, but prior to that she was a division president in a market research firm, which was actually her second career. Directly out of college she won a job with the Rochester Philharmonic Orchestra (RPO) playing oboe, and she successfully pursued an orchestra career for fifteen years. She became interested in business and marketing as a result of a children's book and record that I produced for the RPO in 1984. We had money invested in it, and when the orchestra was slow in responding to the project's marketing needs, Judy stepped in and took it over. It was one of those "seat of the pants" efforts, and we broadened our education as a result. But it paid off, and *My First Concert* sold 15,000 copies, which was considered very good for this type of children's book and record. In fact, it made the *New York Times* list of top gifts for children—Christmas 1984. Judy found great satisfaction in using her creativity to tackle business issues, so she decided to dig deeper and get an MBA (read: Legos). It was during this period that we would talk at the dinner table about her studies. Brands and their importance became an interesting topic of discussion for us, since I already viewed musicians as small businesses and the idea of musicians with identifiable brands made sense to both of us. What follows is a result of those conversations. I give you this background to credit Judy for teaching me about brands.

Some Definitions

What is the first thing you think of when the company Coca-Cola is mentioned—how about Apple or Mercedes? These are all strong brands that have distinct images associated with them. As a musician you also have a brand. You, Inc. means something to those who want to hire you. Let's think about that in business terms for a minute. Put on your business hat again. Here come some definitions.

"A **brand** is a trademark or distinctive name identifying a product or a manufacturer."[9] And **brand equity** is a set of assets and liabilities linked to a brand (name and/or symbol) that add to or subtract from the value provided by a product or service to a firm and/or to that firm's customers.[10] Whew! Even I have to read that last sentence twice! As musicians we don't often think in these terms, but whether intentional or not musicians develop their brands too. Some would call it your reputation or image. Picture a musician like Yo-Yo Ma. What do you think of when you hear his name? It could be—he's at the top of his field, artistic musician, wholesome, diversity, multi-cultural, wide-range of music, personable, good guy, etc. How about Wynton Marsalis? It could be—cultural roots, has respect for the history of jazz music and its preservation, great classical as well as jazz musician, Lincoln Center Jazz, Juilliard, etc. (read: diverse Legos). If Miles Davis is thought of in the same manner it could be—innovative, legendary, cool, hip, bad boy, eccentric, etc.

In business a strong brand is identified with a message or image that is *meaningful to the consumer*. It *stands apart from other brands* and the *consumer feels good* about using it. Marsalis, Ma and Davis are all strong brands. It could be argued that there are other musicians who are equally talented and artistic, but the brand of these three musicians sets them apart from the pack. Some might perceive Davis's brand as having some negative descriptors, but remember what is perceived as negative to some can be positive to others (or reason to go to a concert to see and hear what this person is about).

> **Lesson:**
> Just like companies or products, musicians are brands too.

When people consider going to a Marsalis or Ma concert or purchasing one of their recordings, they base much of their decision on past experiences with these artists. For example, they saw Wynton on television. They liked what they saw and heard, and therefore decided to check him out in a live concert. This potential concert-goer was linking back to past experience in an effort to predict future outcomes. "I like his recordings. I'll like him at a concert. We'll have a good time. Let's buy a ticket."

What Is Your Brand?

Now think about your brand. And it isn't just about your playing, but we can start with that. What do people think of when they think of you? Make a list and write it down. Here's an example of a hypothetical musician.

Good player, great sound, terrific technique, okay sight-reader, inexperienced in orchestra and show work, a little unreliable, no car (you have to give him a ride), can be argumentative. Does this list describe a person you would hire to play a show? Maybe not. His brand has too many negatives, or liabilities. But in reality some of the listed negatives could be based on isolated incidences. The person who views this player as unreliable and argumentative could be basing that on hearsay or on just one observed occurrence.

Musicians who wear several different hats (read: Legos) may be able to extend their brands to adapt to various situations. For example, a person who is a fine composer could also be a great instrumentalist and make violin bows as well. It's possible that some may be familiar with this person only as a composer and have no idea of these other talents.

I hope that it is clear here that the type of good brand building I am talking about is based on good deeds and good playing, both of which occur in an organic sort of way. I'm not talking about a brand that is artificially created by an agency for a movie star, pop-music artist or boy band. I'm talking about the reputation that everyday musicians build over time, as they go about their daily work.

> **Lesson:**
>
> Build your brand on good deeds and good playing.

As previously stated, a strong brand is identified with a message or image that is *meaningful to the consumer, stands apart from other brands* and that *the consumer feels good about using.* Yo-Yo Ma, Wynton Marsalis, Renée Fleming, Paul McCartney, Mick Jagger and Bono are all strong well-known brands. These are the brands of music mega-stars. But, there are also strong brands that are known only by the musicians in a particular subset of the music world. Think of orchestral trombonists, flutists, concertmasters, jazz saxophonists or bassists. Within each small music business subset there are those who stand out above the rest. The musicians in that field know their names. This is true of every community of local musicians, for example in your town or school.

Your brand is built over time and is determined not only by how well you play, but also on how you handle yourself. Recitals, performances and publications all contribute (read: Legos), but even non-musical things play a part in your brand, as well. For example, the people with whom you associate, your appearance, as well as your personality all add to or detract from your brand. It takes a considerable amount of time to build a good brand, but it can be tarnished very quickly with sub-par performance or actions.

> **Lesson:**
>
> Your brand is not only about your playing ability, but in how you handle yourself, too.

It only takes one example of sloppy technique to create doubt in the minds of others regarding your expertise. There is probably truth in the old saying, "You are only as good as your last gig."

It's All about Connection

You've probably heard the cliché, "To get ahead it's not how you play, but who you know." Certainly having connections or a network of friends and acquaintances can help your career, but that's for another part of this book. What we will discuss here, for a moment, is the *manner* in which you connect, or bond, with your audience—the public, other musicians, contractors, conductors, producers, agents, etc. In the end your success will depend upon how well you and your brand bond with your audience, which can be on different levels.[11] It could be that you connect:

> **Cognitively**—They are aware of you and are familiar with your abilities. Do they consider you all the time? Are you the only one they consider? Are you one of many, one of a few or not on their radar screen at all?

> **Behaviorally**—They may consider many, but they always come back to you.

> **Emotionally**—They like you. They've hired you for years. You are friends. Or, they don't like you. They had a run-in with you years ago and have never forgotten it.

> **Fit**—Do your abilities and personality fit the need of the occasion perfectly, somewhat, or not at all? Are you well versed in the style of music required? Do you have a good attitude about playing it?

Brand Image Associations

Your brand exudes a certain image and is made up of the following:

Tangibles and Intangibles[12]

> **Tangible**—Can you play accurately? Do you show up on time? Are you a good sight-reader?

Intangible—Do you have a beautiful sound? Are you musical? Do you make the notes come alive? Do you add something extra with your presence in the group?

Tangible attributes are vulnerable to competition

The tangibles can be competed away. Someone will always play faster, higher and louder, but the intangibles are less vulnerable. If you have an incredibly beautiful, personal sound it is difficult to duplicate. Think of all the top musicians who play your instrument. You can usually identify them upon hearing just a few notes. It's the intangibles—their sound, phrasing, musical idiosyncrasies, the style of music they play and so on that sets them apart.

Points of Parity and Points of Difference[13]

Points of Parity—These are the "must haves" just to be considered at all. They are sometimes called table stakes. Every musician competing for a certain job must have them just to get in the game. For example, if you want to be an orchestra horn player, it is a given that you will be absolutely fluent with transposition.

Points of Difference—These are the things that raise you above the others. Staying with the horn example, if you have a fantastic, never-miss high register and the endurance to go with it, the number of competitors is reduced. You are elevated above the pack.

Know Your Image

This one is important. **Your image lives within the minds of the market, and not within your wishful thinking.** You can try to put forth the image that you want, but your audience (again—co-workers, contractors, conductors, producers, etc.) actually creates that image.

Image, Identity and Positioning—What's the Difference? Image is the impression that the market holds of you. **Identity** is the impression you want to give the market. **Positioning** relates to the elements of Identity that you present to various target audiences.[14] For example, if you are a composer as well as a fine instrumentalist, you might present only your composer side when entering a composition contest. But, when playing a recital you might program one of your own pieces. The important thing is to know your image. What do people associate with you? Is it good? Are you comfortable with it?

> **Lesson:**
>
> Your image is created by your audience. What is your image? Is it good?

Key Measures of Success

The ultimate measures of success are trial and repeat, and the buyer is the final judge. If a manufacturer of just about anything, from dishwashing detergent to automobiles, gets you to try their product, and you are satisfied and return to purchase again, that is success. Using a music example, let's say you get a last minute call to sub on a woodwind quintet educational concert in a high school.

> **Lesson:**
>
> Success is being asked back.

That's your trial. If it goes well you are a hero, even if your playing isn't absolutely flawless. In a last minute situation the other players' expectations are reduced, and they will cut you some slack. They'll be happy to get through the gig without any major train wrecks! But even if you do a great job and impress the other four musicians they might not immediately call you back. There just might not be another opportunity for a while. That quintet already has a permanent member, and as long as he or she continues to do good work, it will remain his or her position. However, the chances are very good that they will recommend you to other groups, or at least relay the story of how you saved the day.

A "Jack of Nothing"–How Diversified Should You Be?

This is always a difficult question to answer and it varies from person to person. It stands to reason that if you do one thing and take it to the max, your chances of being superior to the person who does two or more things is enhanced. With a few exceptions most musicians who are at the absolute top of their field do essentially one thing really, really, really well. Miles Davis didn't have to know anything about the C trumpet or playing the Petrouchka excerpt. Itzhak Perlman doesn't have to know the chord progression of the Blues and Lang Lang doesn't have to play ragtime (though his handlers might have him do that someday). Nevertheless, certain musicians have been able to excel in several diverse areas of music (read: Legos). Leonard Bernstein and Andre Previn immediately come to mind. Wynton Marsalis is arguably another in this elite group.

> **Lesson:**
>
> Strive for breadth and depth in your knowledge and expertise.

Breadth and depth are essential. Take one thing to as high a level as you can as you continue to expand your knowledge and expertise in related areas. But if you stray too far from the core of your brand, believability suffers. Going back to Lang Lang, it could well be that he could become a good ragtime pianist. The music is written out. He has the technique. He would have to capture the style. That is believable, but Lang Lang as a first-class improvising jazz pianist, playing with Joe Lovano isn't. Jazz improvisation is simply too far afield from the Lang Lang brand.

So maintain the core of your brand, and keep it at a high level. It is easy to become a "Jack of Nothing," when you stretch too far to master it all. But that won't happen if you always maintain quality, grow slowly, diversify, hire the best to teach you what you don't know, be flexible and know your competition. We'll talk about these later in the book.

CHAPTER 6

Be Ready for a Non-Linear Career Path

ASK ANY MUSICIAN, whom you consider to be successful, if his career evolved in a straight line and the answer you will probably get is, "No, it didn't." An example of a straight-line career path would be the military. A person who wants to make a life in the military could take R.O.T.C. in high school, attend a service academy, like West Point for college, and upon graduation transition to the Army as a second lieutenant. A straight-line career path has a series of logical "next steps" that typically occur for a large segment of people in that career. But it doesn't work that way with music.

It isn't usual for us to come straight out of college and immediately get plugged into an orchestra job, though it happens now and again. There is always a certain amount of uncertainty in a musician's career, especially in the first few years directly after graduation. But in the course of daily life, friendships are established, acquaintances are made, opportunities present themselves and somehow we put a career together. Flexibility, adaptability and versatility are very important characteristics for a musician to have and to nurture, especially as one enters the profession. It stands to reason that the more things a person does well (Legos) the more employment options are available.

This translates into more channels through which money can flow to put bread on the table.

Probably everyone who has a successful career can look back and say, "I was in the right place at the right time." But is it really luck? Or is it being ready to take advantage of an opportunity that is presented? I recently read a remark by Bob Shieffer, the CBS reporter, made during a commencement address he gave at an area college. I'll paraphrase it here (Schieffer is actually borrowing from Thomas Jefferson here, by the way). Luck plays an important role in your career, but I've observed that the harder I work, the luckier I get. Not that it is that special or unique, but my own career path might provide some insight into that question. As I look back today I find reasons for some of the breaks I've had.

One Person's Story

One of my life goals was, very simply, to have a career in music. I didn't exactly know what it was going to be. At first it was to be a high school band director in my hometown of Denver, Colorado. My musical world was very small. I didn't consider attending any other school except the University of Denver. In fact, I knew very little about any music schools other than the ones in Colorado. I had heard of Juilliard, but that was about it. The DU clarinet teacher and band director at the time, Ralph Strouf, began subtly recruiting me in high school. He offered me several opportunities to play in university groups, which was wonderful for me. I was hanging with the big boys. I wasn't thinking of any future musical opportunities outside of Denver until Mr. Strouf decided to create a National Clarinet Clinic. He brought in well-known teachers and recitalists, and it was there that I met two professors from Michigan State University—Keith Stein and Elsa Ludewig. Not coincidentally Stein had been the teacher of Strouf, and Elsa was the new clarinet *wunderkind* of the time—a fantastic player and teacher. We immediately clicked, and I took advantage of every opportunity to

> **Lesson:**
>
> Take every opportunity to play in master classes. Get noticed.

play for them and learn from their advice. As a result, it was off to MSU to get my master's degree. *(Lesson: If you have the funds, attend summer festivals and camps. Teachers are always on the lookout for talented students, and the connections with other students can pay off down the road too.)*

I started on clarinet at age 10, but took up the saxophone as a secondary instrument at age 16, and played my first "dance job" five weeks later. So, I had an interest playing both classical music and jazz. At Michigan State I wanted to concentrate solely on clarinet, but they had a new major that allowed woodwind players to study all the woodwinds with the exception of saxophone. (That's right, the saxophone was still a bastard child in the '60s.) I had begun flute study as an undergrad, and by then my career aspirations had expanded to include being a freelance, "studio" musician, so this woodwind specialist idea seemed like a good option.

At MSU I continued to work hard on the clarinet, play jazz on the saxophone and ratchet up my proficiency on flute and the double reeds. Elsa was a recently-minted Eastman DMA (Doctor of Musical Arts) graduate. She had nothing but good to say about the School and its clarinet professor, Stanley Hasty. I heard a lot of, "You should go to Eastman," from her, and it began to have an influence on my thinking. I continued to become more sophisticated about music and more open to other viable career possibilities for myself. My musical world was opening up. I saw what Elsa was doing with her career, and I liked it, so I added college professor to my list of job aspirations.

Lesson:

Don't go it alone.
Ask for advice.
Have a mentor,
a confidant.

With Elsa's urging I applied to Eastman for doctorate work and was accepted, but the Vietnam War got in the way. The Army draft was in full operation at that time. I realize it is difficult for many people who didn't live through that period to appreciate what draft-aged men were dealing with. But we knew even then—without the benefit of hindsight and history—that the war was disastrous in

Lesson:

Keep your
network active
and expanding.

every way. Upon graduation from MSU, where my draft status had been 2S (student), it changed to 1A (welcome to the Army). A renewal deferment wasn't guaranteed when one went on to an advanced degree, so I reckoned I was going to be drafted. With the unpopularity of the war, many people my age at the time did anything they could to avoid military service. I didn't want to move to Canada to avoid the draft, so I did some research into possible options, and learned about military bands, which I figured would be a good thing for me, if I could get in. A friend who was ahead of me by one year was in the U.S. Military Academy Band at West Point. I gave him a call and got the low down on military bands. All of a sudden I had another option. In retrospect this is a good illustration of how important your day-to-day connections are. This one quite possibly saved my life!

West Point seemed like a good fit. It was 40 miles from New York City. After basic training, musicians were promoted to the rank of sergeant, and they stayed at West Point for their entire military careers. The commitment was three years instead of four. (The other military branches required a four-year enlistment.) The problem was getting in. At that time West Point was getting about 200 applications a month just to audition! Somehow they let me play for them, but at the audition I was told that they were set on clarinets and saxophones for another year. Could I wait and enlist then? Well, not really. My draft board had other military career opportunities in mind for me! Not good timing.

Lesson:

Versatility creates options. The more things you can do well the greater your options.

But on my application, or possibly in the course of the audition, they saw that I played flute (Legos). I was in luck. If I came in and played piccolo for a year or so in the Field Music unit (fife and drum music), I would transition to the concert band when an opening occurred. It sounded pretty good to me considering the alternative, so I informed Eastman about my draft status and they let me defer enrollment. I would just have to audition for them again when I got out of the Army. Although that's not what I had originally planned, it sounded good to me. After all, plan Z can look pretty good when plans A through Y are out of the picture.

As good as West Point was, it was still the Army. We short-timers didn't want to be there. Most of us were opposed to the war, and we resented that our lives were put on hold. We wouldn't be able to do what we really wanted to do until our military service was over, so we did harmless little things to protest the war. We grew moustaches. After a while the lifers (career military) figured out what was going on. Why are all these guys growing moustaches!? (At that time women were not yet allowed in the band.) It was perfectly within military dress code to have a moustache, but there were very specific rules about its length and appearance. I remember a surprise moustache inspection where all of us scrambled to hurriedly trim things up. Protests aside, in retrospect my three years there were very valuable. My fellow musicians were absolute top-level, and I made many lasting friendships. The Army paid for my lessons in New York City with Leon Russianoff (clarinet) and Albert Regni (flute). And last, but certainly not least, we had a considerable amount of free time, which was great for practicing, and the Catskills and NYC offered excellent playing opportunities. But, it was still the Army.

Three years later with my military service coming to a close, I came to a big decision point. What do I really want to do in life? By then I had my three-pronged attack going—play in an orchestra, freelance on woodwinds in NYC and teach in college. Any of the three were appealing, but the strongest pull for me was to be a teacher in higher education. With that in mind, Eastman seemed like the best opportunity for me. Plus, I had substantial financial aid from them, as well as the G.I. bill, which gave me a check each month to go to school. By then I was married and had an infant

Lesson:

Make the most out of your situation. If you're dealt lemons, make lemonade.

Lesson:

Have a career plan with options built in; recognize hidden opportunities.

daughter. Eastman was too good to pass up, and as destabilizing as the Vietnam War was, my three years in the Army threw many opportunities in my path. Because my career plan was constantly evolving in my mind, I recognized those opportunities for what they were.

I arrived in Rochester, New York, in August, 1970. That was also the starting date of a new Eastman faculty member, Rayburn Wright. For many years Ray had been the music director of Radio City Music Hall. Eastman was looking to expand its jazz offerings and it offered him a position joining Chuck Mangione on the jazz faculty. The department was expanded to two members. Ray taught several levels of jazz composition, arranging and film scoring, and he directed the studio orchestra as well. Because of my background in jazz I was assigned as his graduate

Lesson:

Recognize your mentors and soak up all you can from them.

assistant. It could not have been a more perfect match for me. Ray was the ultimate professional and consummate musician. What a role model and mentor he turned out to be for me! Though I have no way of proving this, I would argue that few people have achieved their dreams in life without at least one mentor who believed wholeheartedly in them. I have been fortunate to have several.

As a doctoral student I wasn't required to play in ensembles, but since I didn't know anyone I figured it would be a good way for me to meet people. In addition, I liked to play. Today Eastman has a rotation system for its large ensembles, but in those days you auditioned and had that position for the year. I was lucky and was given principal clarinet in the Wind Ensemble and lead alto in the Jazz Ensemble (Legos). In retrospect, this was very important for what was to come a couple of years later. Many of my peers chose to lay low and not play in an ensemble. They wanted the extra time to study, but as a consequence they had a very low profile. The students, particularly the

Lesson:

Don't lay low. Get yourself noticed, not by being "pushy," but by doing good work.

undergrads, weren't aware of them. They hadn't made their presence evident. On the other hand, I was interacting with every grade level of student in the school. Not only was I playing in the school groups with them, I was soon playing gigs around town with them.

In the second semester of the second year of my DMA work, one of the clarinet teachers became ill. The reputation (read: brand) I had established that first year served me well. The Eastman administration asked me to take his students and also teach the music education clarinet class. It was the lowest level of applied teaching at Eastman, but I felt like a king. Was I lucky? No question. Was I in the right place at the right time? Absolutely. But this is a good illustration of our trusty Boy Scout pledge: be prepared. Luck can be a factor, but if people know who you are and you have prepared, you'll be ready for opportunities when they arise. It's more than just being in the right place at the right time. It's being prepared and being ready to take it on. As it turned out this teacher never did return to school even though his health improved.

Chuck Mangione was the jazz ensemble director, and in 1970 he was just beginning to gain some national prominence. He had a tremendous following in Rochester. Our school jazz ensemble concerts regularly filled the 3,000-plus seats of the Eastman Theatre. And outside of Eastman, Chuck was putting together concerts and record albums that featured his quartet and studio orchestra. The scoring of his music included saxophones with lots of flute doubles. I'm glad I decided to play in the school jazz ensemble. From that experience Chuck knew what I could do (my Legos). He hired me to play on several of his albums, including *Bellavia,* a 1977 Grammy award winner, and to tour with the expanded group. I did this throughout the '70s until he went totally with the quartet format.

Lesson:

Show people what you can do. Do more than what is expected.

Toward the end of the 1971–72 school year, Chuck's star was rising, and his popularity continued to grow even more. He wanted Eastman to make a stronger commitment to him, but the school wasn't ready for that. Chuck, who was never shy in his demands or convictions, opted out and abruptly left just one or two weeks before the start of the 1972–73 school year. For me—right place-right time? I guess so, because I was asked to direct the second jazz ensemble, teach improvisation and continue to teach clarinet. All I had left on the DMA was the dissertation, so it seemed manageable to me. This was a one-year position, but the following year (1973–74) I was offered a three-year contract and a faculty appointment—Instructor in Clarinet. At that time it was made clear to me that a tenure track position was probably not in the cards. Fine. I was happy with what I had, and I had three years to show them how indispensible I was and what a good deal they had.

By this time, two prongs of my three-pronged plan were in place— teach at the college level and play freelance, studio gigs. The third was to come in September 1974 when I auditioned for and won the third clarinet/bass clarinet job with the Rochester Philharmonic Orchestra. I was not unknown by the musicians of the RPO. I had been a soloist with them on a new music piece in 1972 and had also done some subbing with them. In September 1974 an

Lesson:

Don't let your head destroy your confidence.

opening came up and I began to prepare myself for the audition, but a week or so before I started getting cold feet. The excerpts weren't going as well as I wanted, and I began to lose confidence in my abilities. The *Daphnis and Chloe* bass clarinet excerpt was my nemesis. I got it maybe 80 percent of the time, and that wasn't good enough. My head got in the way, too. Now that I was an official "Eastman professor" what would happen if a student beat me out! How would that look! What would people think! My head won the battle. I decided not to audition, and I notified the RPO that I wouldn't compete for the open position.

On the day of the audition I was in my studio at school practicing when I got a call from the principal clarinetist, Michael Webster. "Ray, we're down here at the audition and we haven't heard anyone we like. Can you come here and play for us?" I was shocked! This is not the way these things usually happen! I said okay and off I went to the audition location that was a few blocks from school. On the way over

I was thinking, "I have nothing to lose. If I screw up I can say it was because I hadn't played the excerpts for two weeks." Suddenly my head was working in my favor, rather than against me, like before.

The only members of the audition committee I remember being at the audition were David Zinman, the newly appointed music director, Isaiah Jackson the assistant conductor and the principal and second clarinetists of the orchestra (Michael Webster and Stan Gaulke). Long story short—it was the best audition I ever played in my life! Everything fell into place. I was very relaxed and just had a good time. It felt like those movies when the pool player starts running the table and everything is dropping one after another—no questions and absolutely no doubt about anything. The third prong was in place. I had my orchestra job. This was a huge lesson for me: when you play, it's important to try to relax and have fun. You know you've prepared as much as time would allow, so try to let the "flow" carry you. (P.S.: This is easy to say but can be hard to do.)

Lesson:

Don't psych yourself out. When you play, try to relax and have fun.

Fast-forward two years to 1976. Knowing that I played saxophone as well as clarinet (Legos), some students began requesting me for secondary lessons. Since a common conversation topic around any music school is about lessons and teachers, the saxophone majors (still in small numbers at the time) heard about some of the things my students were working on in their lessons. Another long story short—nearly the entire saxophone class of my colleague went to the administration and asked to transfer to my studio. The academic dean listened and suddenly the roles were reversed. I taught the saxophone majors and my colleague taught the secondaries.

Lesson:

Don't minimize the importance of word-of-mouth information, or the effect it can have on your brand.

We will leave this career journey down memory lane with 30 years still remaining to tell. The points have been made, I think:

- Have options
- Have a plan *(it doesn't have to, probably shouldn't, be cast in stone)*
- Work hard
- Prepare for what you want to do in life
- Build your brand
- Find some mentors and listen to them
- Show people what you can do
- Don't psych yourself out

Your Mission

This is something I never thought about until I was asked to serve on a committee to review and update the mission statement of the Eastman School. We went back and forth wordsmithing and shaping the document. Much thought went into it, and the new statement certainly wasn't created overnight. A mission statement is an important unifying document for both profit and not-for-profit organizations. They are created to define the organization and its purpose. Here is one example—the mission statement of the Eastman School of Music.

- To give the student an intensive professional education in his or her musical discipline.
- To prepare each student with a solid foundation in music and an expansive education in the liberal arts.
- To develop an informed and inquiring mind that enables each graduate to engage the fundamental issues of his or her art and to become an effective cultural leader in society.
- And, through its community and continuing education programs, to offer the highest quality music instruction and performance opportunities for students of all ages.

For Eastman these bullets boil down to **performance, scholarship, leadership** and **community,** which is easy to remember.

Mission statements are also used as yardsticks with which to measure the worth of a new idea that may be presented. New ideas and opportunities can be weighed against the mission. It either fits or it doesn't. It's either in or out. For example, if the Eastman School were presented with an opportunity to expand into the field of dance, it would not be a fit because the school's mission is to give a professional education in music. Of course mission statements can be changed, and the fact is they are often reviewed and tweaked, but their core values generally stay the same.

With this semi-boring discussion of mission statements behind us you may be asking yourself, "This is good for businesses and music schools, but what does that have to do with me. I just want to play the trumpet."

Ask yourself these questions:

Why do I want a life in music (teach, perform, compose, do scholarly work, sing, etc.), and is the world a better place because of my doing this?

If your answer is, "I perform because it brings me great joy to share my musical talent with others," you are probably in the right profession. If your answer is, "I like to travel and I think it would be fun to play in a band," you might want to think about how much fun that traveling band might be when you are 60 years old. Here is an example of a talented person who had a successful music career but found it personally frustrating and unfulfilling.

Jason was a talented student who was a standout jazz musician from his early high school days. At age 14 everyone said this kid was destined to be something special. He majored in music in college, went on to tour with a major jazz artist and got his master's degree in jazz performance. Almost immediately out of graduate school he landed a college job teaching jazz studies. All seemed perfect, but throughout his first three years of college teaching, the frustration grew to be unbearable. This, combined with family difficulties, led him to resign his position and return to his hometown. His plan was to freelance in the medium size market and open a small project-recording studio. After a couple of years he decided 24/7 music wasn't for him anymore, so he took a day gig and is now a Senior Analyst with a Fortune 70 corporation. He continues to regularly play and record, and still sounds great.

What was the source of the frustration that made him give up a seemingly good life doing music full time? He explained to me that as a child he had a very turbulent home life. There was a lot of tension between his parents, with arguing and verbal abuse, and there wasn't much attention and validation given to him. As a result he went into an escape mode. He practiced all the time, putting in endless hours not only to drown out the turmoil around him, but because practicing gave him a sense of accomplishment and confidence, especially as he started to excel at music. Further, performing in front of an audience that appreciated him gave him the feeling that he had value.

Lesson:

Discover your *raison d'être.* What is your life's mission?

He was a great high school player, so it was logical to go to college and major in music. But doing so created the ultimate paradox. By studying music so intensely throughout college he had set the standard so high for himself that he could never live up to it. The joy and sense of accomplishment was gone. This came to a head most dramatically after a performance with a New York A-List musician who complimented Jason on his playing. He simply couldn't believe this respected musician actually meant what he said. In Jason's own mind (based on what he had learned), he did not live up to his own standards and was therefore not worthy of any such compliment.

In spite of this, he continued on a music career path until his frustration grew so great that he woke up one day and said to himself, "I've been doing this for the wrong reasons. I need to do something else." He found that his "mission" really wasn't about helping students learn or sharing the beauty of music with others. He had used music as an escape all his life, and years after he was out of his parents' house and on his own, the escape was no longer necessary. Further, the music that provided the escape was no longer fulfilling for him. That was then, and this is now: I am happy to report that after coming to that realization, today music for Jason is once again very fulfilling and is no longer a source of frustration for him.

I think it's useful to give yourself a reality check from time to time. What is your purpose in life? The French have a phrase for it—*raison d'être*, reason for being or your reason for existence. Just think about your mission and why you do what you do. Ask yourself questions like, "Why am I doing this?" "Am I happy doing this?" "Can I picture myself doing anything else?" "Am I just going through the motions, or am I really getting the most out of my talent and ability?" "I'm here at point A. I want to be at point B. How do I get there?" "What is my *raison d'être?*"

Your Five-Year Career Plan

Let's get some things on the table. An idea is just an idea until it is written down. Plans are good. But . . . Did I have a five-year plan in high school? Well, sort of. Was it anything like what I ended up doing in my career? No. Did it morph as I matured and became aware of other opportunities? Yes, without a doubt. Was it written down? Are you kidding? But was it thought through? Yes, by the time I was in graduate school it was. Do I have a plan today? Of course! Is it written down? Of course not, I'm human, but do as I say, and not as I do. I'm going to suggest that you put some things on paper.

Plans are good. If you want to build just about anything you need a plan. They organize your thoughts and help you to think through whatever you are trying to do. Think about building a house. You don't do the roof before you do the walls and you don't build the walls before the foundation is set. If you want it to look good and not fall down in the first windstorm you need a plan—a blueprint. In a similar manner in which you build a house, you can create a blueprint for your career. And you don't have to be stuck with it for life. It will morph and change over time as some doors open and others close. The good thing is that it compels you to think about what you have accomplished thus far in life, where you want to be and how you propose to get there. What

> **Lesson:**
>
> Have a plan. Write it down. Check back on it from time to time. Make adjustments.

follows is an exercise I use as part of my Entrepreneurial Thinking class at the Eastman School. It's simple and there are no right or wrong answers.

For many, especially younger players, their goal in music is often "to get better." That's a perfectly good answer for them. But, if they decide to make a life in music they will very soon be faced with figuring out how to survive and thrive as a professional. The purpose of this exercise is to give you the opportunity to assess your strengths and weaknesses and to think about some possible career paths. In simple terms, *"What do you see yourself doing five years from now?"* (If you are in high school or a college student begin your five-year plan after receiving your degree.)

1. Your plan should include an objective and how much you expect to be paid. For example: "Play trumpet with the national touring company of a Broadway show." Or: "Play viola in the Chicago Symphony." Here is an example for the viola player. Move to Chicago. Take some lessons with the principal or associate principal violist of the CSO. Weasel into some community orchestras. Study the repertoire. Get your audition chops up by taking auditions. Try to get on the CSO sub list. Wait for someone to die. Be accepted for an audition. Beat the other two hundred people out.

2. What is your comparative advantage over others? What is it about you (musically and personally) that makes you better than others going for the same gig? What are your weaknesses? For example, here are some possible strengths. You've studied with the CSO Principal Violist. You've even subbed with them once. Weakness: Your instrument is not very good.

3. What are the outside factors that could stand in your way—factors over which you have no control? For instance, there could be no viola opening in the Chicago Symphony during the time period that you are considering. (The purpose of this

question is to get you to think about what could happen. Be reasonable. Don't include, "I break my hand," etc.)

4. What are some things you can do to overcome these outside factors? For example, you want to be a freelance session player but you see that the business is shrinking due to the use of synthesizers, computers and electronics. Answer—Learn about synthesizers, computers and electronics.

5. List your alternative strategies with evaluation and estimates of likelihood. (What are your options?) How about another strategy? The violist could take every orchestra audition that presents itself. Gain experience. Keep ties to the CSO through his or her already established contacts. Wait for an opening and a chance to audition. Here is still another idea. Apply to a Chicago area music school to work on a graduate degree. What a bonus if the viola teacher happens to play in the CSO. Maybe something will open up, but at least you will have a master's degree in two years that may prepare you for a teaching position as well.

6. Decision: selection of preferred strategy and rationale for your choice. (Why you chose this objective.)

I like to think of a career in music as a journey—a road trip. Let's say you want to get to Joe's Crab Shack in Boise, Idaho. You live in Rochester, New York. You know that Idaho is west of Rochester so at the outset you could simply get in your car and drive west. You wouldn't need a map—yet. But there will come a time in your westward travel that you will have to ask directions or look at a map. There is a lot of territory in the West and just to find the state you need guidance. Without good information you could over or undershoot by a thousand miles, or worse yet wander around aimlessly hoping "something will come up." If you get lucky and do make it to Boise, the fun will really begin, because Joe's Crab Shack is someplace in that city but you have no idea where.

Compare this to your life in music. At the outset it's okay to simply head west. If you are getting better and gaining experience all is good, but as you get older and begin to home in on what you want to do for the next several years, a map or plan will help you. You won't be married to it and it can change. What it will do is get you thinking about what you want to do with music in your life.

CHAPTER 7

Seven Things That Will Help You Make Money

Effectively Articulating Your Idea

As previously stated in this book, an idea is just an idea until it is written down. Obviously getting your thoughts down on paper is essential if you are going to present it to others (read: ask for money), but it is also critical as an aid to help you think the project through. For example: if you are contemplating making a recording you need a concept, design, art work, other musicians, studio time, engineer, etc. This all costs money. Before you embark on the project it is good to know what your break-even point will be, and how many CDs or downloads you will need to sell before you start making a profit.

A business plan is a detailed description and explanation that serves as a guide or blueprint over the lifetime of the business. It addresses the questions of Who, What, When, Where, Why, How and How Much. It is comprehensive and includes marketing and operational plans as well

> **Lesson:**
>
> An idea is just an idea until it is written down.

as detailed financials. If you want to start a business you need a business plan for both you and anyone or any entity that you will ask for financing.

Another tool for evaluating ideas, projects, concepts, etc., is called a SWOT analysis. Albert Humphrey at Stanford University developed it during the 1960s, and its name is derived from the first letter of each parameter it addresses—Strengths, Weaknesses, Opportunities and Threats. It is also a useful tool in thinking through projects. Information on both business plans and SWOT analysis is readily available on the Internet and interested persons can reference them there.

In my own work I have used a set of questions to help me articulate ideas ranging from new degree programs to ideas for books. I arrived at these with the help of my wife who is a successful business executive, and I've found them particularly useful and effective when presenting ideas to others. To a typical MBA business person I'm sure they will seem elementary, naïve and even common knowledge, but if you went to music school this will be new to you!

Questions to Ask Yourself and Answer When Organizing and Articulating Your Idea (Project, Course, New Degree, Chamber Series, Tour, Recording, Business, etc.)

- Overview   What is the idea? (1–2 paragraphs stated succinctly)

- Rationale   Why is it needed? (1–2 paragraphs)

- What are the benefits?
  - To the customers
  - To the musical community
  - To the community in general
    - Local
    - National

- What is unique about it?

- Does it serve a want or a need?

- What are the industry dynamics?
  - Market Trends

- ○ Market Size
- ○ Competition: direct and indirect
- ○ Barriers to entry
- ○ Competitive threats

- • Who are my customers?
  - ○ Where are they located?
  - ○ Projected size of the market
  - ○ What are their needs?
  - ○ How can I meet their needs?

- • What will it cost me to produce it?
  - ○ All expenses thought through carefully
  - ○ My time
  - ○ What is the break even point?

- • How long will it take to produce it?
  - ○ Make a timeline

- • How will I market it?
  - ○ Do some research

- • Are people willing to pay for this idea, product or talent?
  - ○ What can I charge?
  - ○ What do others charge for similar products?

By going through this process you will have a better understanding of your idea and its feasibility. You may discover that you can't make enough money to undertake the project. It is better to find that out before you get fully involved, rather than somewhere down the road in the middle of the project.

Making a Professional-Sounding Recording

As a musician it is an absolute must to have a top quality recording that is representative of what you do. It's your calling card. The first step is the recording itself and the second step is the way in which you will store and deliver it—CD, DVD Audio, Mp3 file, MIDI file, etc. Let's walk through the process.

What Is the Intended Purpose?

Is it to document your work—your senior recital for example? Is it a demo for certain types of gigs, like wedding ceremonies, wedding parties, jazz clubs, graduate school applications or cruise ship gigs? Recordings for these purposes are important and you should definitively make them, but they are different from projects that you hope will fill a gap in the literature by focusing on a niche market.

> **Lesson:**
>
> A professional-sounding recording is a musician's business card.

If your music is "classical," consider overlooked or unusual instrumentation or secondary or neglected composers. The second group is more appealing to record labels. They already have a zillion versions of the standard repertory in their catalogues. Another version of the Mozart Concerto for your instrument is perfectly acceptable on your demo CD, but not very interesting to a company that hopes to make money on your recording. The standard repertory has been mined and there "ain't much gold left in them thar catalogues."

If your purpose is to put your name on the map and to contribute something to the repertory of your instrument and to the recorded literature, look for the spaces or gaps in the major catalogues. If your music is "non-classical" (i.e., jazz, folk, cross-over, R&B, Christian, etc.) have some tunes that can be played on the radio—five minutes or less.

Who Is Your Audience, and How Do You Get to Them?

Several years ago I did a "sweetening" session (overdubbing horn and string section parts over previously recorded rhythm tracks) for a Christian instrumentalist. The arrangements were hipped up versions of hymns. I was thinking, "These are fun to play. They really groove. The artist is excellent, but who will buy them?" I guess I didn't have my entrepreneur hat on that day. As I talked to the producer, he enlightened me. The artist for whom we were doing the session was a music minister who, in addition to his own church job, did guest appearances at other churches. He sells his CDs at those events. But the big *Ah-ah* came to me when he told me that there are more than 2,400 Christian radio stations in the U.S., and apparently they are always interested in new material. The music was from the public domain, which meant that the copyright was free and clear, so there would be royalties for the arranger and/or soloist involved too. This musician had identified his market.

Do your own research. Maybe there are mailing lists available for your target audience. The Internet makes quick research so easy today.

Steps in the Process

There are books devoted to all aspects of the recording process that are easily found on Amazon.com and elsewhere, but here are a few general things to consider when getting started.

- Come up with a concept
  - ○ Have a theme for the album and select the repertory, then put it through the "Effectively Articulating Your Idea" section of this book.

- Make a budget
  - ○ Do the research and get estimates. Begin by "ball-parking" the figures that you don't know yet, and fill in the hard numbers as you get them. This will give you an idea of what you are getting into. Envision the "Cadillac" model first. If money or time were no object, what would your project look like? If it comes in at more than you can afford, find ways to reduce expenses while maintaining a high quality. Pare it down to the "Chevrolet" version. If you were putting a new roof on your house you wouldn't sign with the first person who gave you a price. Get several different quotes.
  - ○ When the numbers are in, calculate the break-even point of the project. This tells you how many units you have to

sell to get your money back. Here's an example using round numbers for a project that will cost $8,000 with 1,000 CDs produced.

Total cost of the project ($8,000), divided by the number of units manufactured (1,000) equals $8 per unit. If sold at $16, the total possible revenue is $16,000 (16 x 1,000). Divide $16 into $8,000 (the amount invested) and that yields about 500, the number of CDs that need to be sold at $16 to get your money back. Everything above that is gravy.

- Choose the musicians and pay them fairly
  - o Consider an established special guest with name recognition for some of the tracks. Your friends are a good resource too, but make sure they can deliver the goods.

- Find a producer
  - o The producer's responsibilities can range from functioning as another set of ears in the control booth to helping in all aspects of the project. At the minimum, in addition to the engineer, always have a second set of ears in the booth. Engineers are generally better at catching technical problems than musical ones, and the performing musicians, when listening to playback, often focus on their own parts. A good producer sees the forest as well as the trees and can be of great value in keeping the session moving along.

- Find a studio
  - o Word of mouth recommendations are always helpful. Visit their location and acquire some samples. What equipment do they provide—drum kit, piano, etc.? Is the piano good enough for what you need to record? What is the hourly rate? Are package deals or off-hour rates available? Does your project need a fancy studio? Will there be overdubbing? Would a recital hall or church be appropriate for what you need to do?

- The session
  - Have the music thoroughly rehearsed prior to the actual session. Have a performance or two under your belt and the bugs worked out. (Note: This never happens on commercial dates. It's always just show up and find out what is in store for you.)
  - Be prepared and organized. Have a schedule. Make efficient use of both the musicians' and studio's time.

- Editing, mixing, mastering
  - Much of this can be done in a home studio environment if you have the right software such as Pro Tools. Use comparison albums and make sure to listen to the playback on several different systems. You might find that the great bass sound you were getting in the studio is absent when played over your car speakers.

- Photography, art, liner notes, album design
  - If you are self-publishing, simply search the web for "CD design templates," and you will find a plethora of information. Discmakers.com is particularly useful. A rule of thumb from vinyl record days was to avoid photographs on the cover, since they can date the product. Those bell-bottoms and tie-dyed t-shirts are a dead give-away. That is probably still good advice today.

- Take care of legal issues
  - Obtain the rights for the compositions (Harry Fox Agency); copyright your work (copyright.gov); sign-up with ASCAP, BMI or SESAC; consider starting a publishing company. For all of the above see the section on Royalties that follows in this chapter.

- Find a manufacturer
  - A web search of "CD duplication" will produce literally millions of sites from which to choose. Your producer and/or the recording studio will undoubtedly have some suggestions of manufacturers in your area. Get some estimates.

- Distribution—finding a label
    - Here again, the web makes it incredibly easy to obtain lists of record companies. The site, allrecordlabels.com has a database of more than 24,000 record label websites. You can browse by genre, format, city or country, but it's almost too much information. Your best bet is to research CDs that publish your genre of music. What companies keep coming up over and over? Who is putting out the quality product? Talk to friends, teachers and associates who have CDs out there and find out if they are happy with their label. They might even be willing to make a call on your behalf.

- Self-distribution
    - Prior to the emergence of the web, self-distribution was very difficult for the average person. There just wasn't access to the distribution channels that the record labels had. You could sell your record locally but that was about it. Today, through your website, Facebook, MySpace and other social networking sites, along with companies like CDBaby, Amazon and ArtistShare® it is possible to get your music to a wider, albeit niche, audience. Panos Panay, founder and CEO of Sonicbids, has summed up the situation very well, "The Internet has been like the French Revolution for the music business . . . The aristocracy 'has faded' as the cost of distribution, production and even getting connected has come down." Now he adds, "anyone with a niche or devoted fans can make a living."[15]
    - Maria Schneider, who is profiled later in this book, is the poster child for jazz CD self-distribution. Her 2005 CD *Concert in the Garden* was released only through her ArtistShare® website, and became the first Grammy-winning recording with Internet-only sales ("Best Large Ensemble Album"). She repeated her Grammy-winning ways in 2007 with "Best Instrumental Composition," *Cerulean Skies*. She is certainly evidence that

it is possible to be successful doing self-distribution, but success like this doesn't come automatically. She works hard at it and she is also extremely talented.

Vanity Publishing

In the book-publishing world there are companies who will print and bind a book at the author's expense, and the finished books are the property of the author. There is little or no quality control. You supply the manuscript and they do the rest. In other words, anything can be "published" if you are willing to pay for it. These companies are referred to as vanity publishers or vanity presses. There are similar companies in the sound-recording world. Below is a contract that a fledgling saxophone quartet of former students brought to me to look over and to advise them. The company's business is in classical music. It is a small label, but you see their product around. The names have been changed to protect the guilty. My comments are in italics.

Date

This contract is entered into by and between A PROFESSIONAL SAXOPHONE QUARTET, hereinafter referred to as the PERFORMERS, and REALLY-GOOD RECORDS, INC., a Mississippi Corporation.

1. The PERFORMERS will supply REALLY-GOOD RECORDS with a fully edited digital production of one (1) ALBUM. The ALBUM will consist of works by Dana Wilson, Pierne, Faure, Von Koch, Bozza, Joplin, Gillespie, Glenn Miller, Rimsky-Korsakov, and additional works to be determined by the mutual consent of the PERFORMERS and REALLY-GOOD RECORDS, performed by the PERFORMERS. The master tape must be in the 1610/1630 format, or it must be a DAT conforming to the standards set forth in REALLY-GOOD RECORDS' Specifications for DAT Masters' sheet. The master tape must be recorded by an engineer who is approved in advance by REALLY-GOOD RECORDS.

This means that the recording company puts up no money to record the CD.

2.   The PERFORMERS will provide the amount of five thousand five hundred dollars ($5,500.00) to REALLY-GOOD RECORDS, to be used toward the production of the ALBUM in the compact disc format. This amount must be remitted to REALLY-GOOD RECORDS within a period of thirty days of the date that REALLY-GOOD RECORDS receives the master tape. This must take place within a period not to exceed twelve months from the date of this contract.

Not only does the quartet have to supply a finished, ready-to-press master, they also have to pay REALLY-GOOD to manufacture it!

3.   The PERFORMERS will be responsible for all costs associated with the production of the master tape.

That was already spelled out in numbers 1 and 2 above, but REALLY-GOOD is taking no chances for misunderstanding.

4.   REALLY-GOOD RECORDS will pay all expenses other than those listed in item numbers one (1), two (2), and three (3) above that are necessary in order to produce and release the ALBUM in the compact disc format.

There aren't many expenses remaining!

5.   The PERFORMERS warrant that the performers included on this ALBUM will not re-record for commercial release any of the music contained in this recording (except for REALLY-GOOD RECORDS) for a period of five years after the release of this recording. This does not preclude the performers from recording the music for broadcast-only purposes.

Okay.

6. REALLY-GOOD RECORDS will coordinate all further activities necessary to produce the ALBUM in the compact disc format.

Okay.

7. REALLY-GOOD RECORDS will coordinate the distribution of the ALBUM and promotion activities.

Okay.

8. If additional units of the ALBUM are manufactured following the initial production run, REALLY-GOOD RECORDS will pay for such manufacturing. This includes the cost of the discs, booklets and any other costs incurred in such manufacturing.

Okay, but this project will probably never get to that point.

9. For all units of the ALBUM covered by this contract that are sold in the United States, REALLY-GOOD RECORDS will pay to the PERFORMERS a royalty equal to 10 percent of the amount that REALLY-GOOD RECORDS receives from its distributors for each unit, for every unit sold, minus returns. For all units of the ALBUM that are sold outside of the United States, REALLY-GOOD RECORDS will pay to the PERFORMERS a royalty equal to 5 percent of the amount that REALLY-GOOD RECORDS receives from its distributors for each unit, for every unit sold, minus returns. In the event that REALLY-GOOD RECORDS sells any units directly to retail outlets or to final customers, they will be counted as having been sold at the then prevailing REALLY-GOOD RECORDS price to distributors in the United States. A unit is defined as having been sold upon receipt of payment for the unit by REALLY-GOOD RECORDS. Applicable

royalties will be paid by REALLY-GOOD RECORDS to one person or organization designated by the PERFORMERS.

This is very bad for the quartet. "REALLY-GOOD will pay . . . a royalty equal to 10 percent of the amount that REALLY-GOOD RECORDS receives from its distributors for each unit." This is a round-about way of saying 10 percent of wholesale. The distributers buy CDs from REALLY-GOOD at the wholesale price—most likely at a discount of 40 to 60 percent of retail price. The quartet should go for retail price.

10. The PERFORMERS will once annually be sent a report disclosing the number of ALBUM units sold during the prior annual period. Applicable royalties will be sent with the reports.

Most often it is twice a year.

11. The PERFORMERS will provide REALLY-GOOD RECORDS with notes about the musical compositions to be included with the ALBUM. REALLY-GOOD RECORDS may edit these notes as needed.

Okay.

12. REALLY-GOOD RECORDS will have complete rights to the recordings, and will own the session tapes, master tapes, all mastering parts, and all graphic materials related to this ALBUM. Any sale or licensing to another company of the ALBUM is subject to the terms set forth in this contract.

This is very bad for the quartet. REALLY-GOOD will have virtually no money invested yet they want to own everything.

13. The PERFORMERS may purchase units of the ALBUM in the compact disc format from REALLY-GOOD RECORDS.

The cost for such units will be multiples of 25 units, the 25 units representing the minimum order. The PERFORMERS may not sell any units to distributors or to retail or mail order outlets. No royalties will be paid to the PERFORMERS for units that they purchase from REALLY-GOOD RECORDS. REALLY-GOOD RECORDS may adjust this price if it deems necessary after the ALBUM has been on the market for a period of two years.

The price for the CDs is not stipulated. It should be the wholesale price or less, and why should no royalties be paid?

14. REALLY-GOOD RECORDS may, at its discretion, release the ALBUM in any additional mechanical format(s) (i.e., digital audio cassette, cassette, etc.), subject to all of the terms set forth in this contract, with the exception that the PERFORMERS will not provide any funding toward such release.

This is very generous of them. They won't charge the quartet again.

15. If for any reason REALLY-GOOD RECORDS removes this title from its active catalogue for a period exceeding twelve months, the master tapes and all rights to the recording will revert to the PERFORMERS.

This is good for the quartet as far as the recording is concerned, but there is no provision for the art-work, liner notes, design, etc.

16. REALLY-GOOD RECORDS will complete the CDs within a period of six months of receiving all of the necessary materials from the PERFORMERS.

Good.

17. This agreement has been entered into in the State of Mississippi, and the validity, interpretation and legal effect

of this agreement shall be governed by the laws of the State of Mississippi.

John

        Herbie Needleman
        REALLY-GOOD RECORDS, Inc.

Paul

George

Ringo
The PERFORMERS

In the contract there is no mention of mechanical rights. (For an explanation see the section on Royalties that follows in this chapter.) Some of the selections are in the public domain, but several are under copyright. REALLY-GOOD RECORDS is either ignoring their obligation to pay the mechanical rights, or they are just not saying anything about that in the contract. Most likely they are hoping that the quartet will not be savvy enough to ask about them, and that the company will collect the royalties.

> **Lesson:**
>
> Be careful when asked to sign any contract. You must understand it.

I counseled the quartet to pass on this contract and they did. It doesn't take a high-powered lawyer to advise us that this contract is totally biased toward the record label. But, there are obviously some musicians who agree to this type of agreement, because this label does have a fairly extensive catalogue. In addition to paying to publish, a further downside is that the record label carries with it absolutely no prestige.

A further comment is necessary. Even if you think you understand a contract, it is wise to have a lawyer look it over before you sign. What I have done in the past to save time and expense is to ask my lawyer to review the contract with particular attention to items that I didn't understand. There is further record label discussion in Chapter 9.

Getting Gigs

Getting gigs is reasonably easy to do. Getting gigs that pay enough to support you can be a little more difficult. Gigs come in all different shapes and sizes. There are gigs that you do for experience (read: they don't pay very well, but could lead to something better down the road). There are gigs you do for fun, like playing a jam session at a local club. There are others you do because you are passionate about the music or group—for example, your chamber group or your band. Still others you do for the money. Hopefully you don't do many just for the money. The music business is largely based on referral. Someone recommends you to someone else. If you recognize this, it makes sense that the more people you know who do the same kind of work as you, the more opportunities you have to be recommended for a particular job. It's patently obvious. You must get your name around. And in order for that to happen you must build a network of professional contacts. How does one begin? Here are some ideas for those just getting started in the professional world.

The most important thing you must do, especially when you are playing with people you have never met before, is to do a good job. That goes without saying. Secondly, don't be a wallflower. Introduce yourself and be personable. You don't have to overdo it. Just be friendly. As you meet and work with more people, your network will begin to expand. Find out who the main contractors are in the area and contact them. Offer to send them a recording and a résumé. It won't happen overnight, but in time you will begin to get busy.

> **Lesson:**
>
> Get your name around. Network.

When I was younger I would play any kind of music. I didn't want to take a "day-gig" working part-time at a bank or waiting tables. I wanted to be a full-time musician, and I figured that anytime I was playing I could be gaining experience. That philosophy worked for me, but those were the days of six-nights-a-week gigs.

As you get older the name of the game is getting better work that 1) pays more and 2) is more musically satisfying. Just as the all-county band reference on your résumé is not so important when you are in your thirties, you also phase out playing entry level gigs. Cruise ship houseband gigs are good for those just out of school, but not many of us want to devote our lives to that lifestyle. However, a two-to-three-week gig playing in a so-called "celebrity band" can be a very good, paid vacation.

If you have a small ensemble such as a string quartet, woodwind or brass quintet, or a jazz group, you need gigs to keep the players interested, motivated and working toward something. If you are in the musician's union there are "trust-fund jobs" that are doled out by union officials, though funding for them has been considerably reduced of late. You can inquire about these at your local union office. Another possibility is Young Audiences, which is the first and largest arts-in-education network in the U.S. It does many things to promote arts-in-education, and one of them is to connect and provide various arts performances to schools. See if there is an office in your community. Whether it is Young Audiences or a similar organization under a different name in your area, the schools are a good source for small group performance opportunities.

On your own you can find out which schools have good music programs and then contact the band or orchestra directors. Offer to have your group come to their school to play for the music students and to work with their students in a sectional or master class format. Keep your price low. These are usually very easy performance opportunities to get.

Lesson:

To get a gig sometimes all you have to do is ask.

It sounds silly, but when trying to book your own group, sometimes all you have to do is ask. You must be pro-active. Sit down with your group or band and put your heads together. Make a list of potential places that might possibly be interested in hiring you. Armed with a good recording and some information about the group, go to the venue and ask to speak to the manager. Be dressed appropriately for the place you are visiting. (Hint: If you are pitching your punk-rock band to play at a bar, you don't have to be wearing a suit!)

Each person in your group has contacts back home and they can be good resources for you. Talk to your old band directors. If you can get one anchor gig, you can then build around it. Filling in with school concerts is easy to set up. It's possible to do a couple of these a day. Again, keep the price low, and remember that you'll be gaining experience, regardless of where you play. Let's face it, playing a short concert and talking with the students is a lot better than sitting in your hotel room watching TV.

Today the Internet is really your best and cheapest way to introduce yourself to someone who may want to hire your group. Get your website together. It is your digital portfolio and probably the first thing a potential employer will see. You'll need a group bio, a few photos and some representative recordings available for downloading. But even in this world of Internet-speed and easy contact, nothing is more important than having a network of human contacts—friends or mentors who can send an introductory email or make a phone call on your group's behalf. Make friends. Expand your network.

In this section I've been talking about entry-level performance opportunities. Once you get your feet wet you will find your own path as you meet people, play different styles of music, get older and gain experience. Remember—you can direct this journey. It doesn't have to be rambling. You don't have to aimlessly wander in the desert. Keep your focus on where you want to go, and plot out the necessary steps to get there.

Setting Up a Private Teaching Studio

Many things can seem simple when you look from the outside in, but when you actually get into the situation, you find that there is much more than you thought. That's what I used to think about teaching private lessons at home. Students come to your house. You give them a lesson. They give you money. But my experience with one-on-one teaching was coming from a conservatory setting. I've taught studio lessons at Eastman for nearly 40 years. All the details are taken care of by the school. I have an office, a salary and access to the library. I don't have to worry about being paid and if a student cancels it is his/her responsibility to find a rescheduled time. I don't have to put together or schedule recitals. I have no liability issues because the school has insurance. The private studio teacher, on the other hand, does have to think about these things. I'm not talking about the college music student who has two or three younger students and either meets them at school or goes to their home to give the lessons. I'm talking about the person who wants to maintain a professional stature but teach from his or her home.

> **Lesson:**
>
> Successful private studio teachers are organized and professional.

Market Research

Let's say that your main career objective is to be the best possible private teacher in a given area and you are willing to live anywhere. How would you decide where to live? I'd say it's time for some market research. So turn on your computer.

For each city or town on your list of possible destinations, or even if you are simply going to stay where you are, you have access to a great deal of information through the web. Visit the Chamber of Commerce websites as well as the city and county sites. Start with the population. Is it rising? How about the surrounding suburbs? What are the demographics of the area? How many school-age children? What levels? Are the public school music programs thriving? What about other artistic or cultural outlets—museums, theatres? How about higher education? Is there a college with a music school in the community? Do they have a recital series? What about the cost of living and the unemployment

> **Lesson:**
>
> Test your ideas with research.

rate? These questions can be readily answered from your computer. From this information you will be able to make some assumptions about the feasibility of making a living as a studio teacher in a particular location.

Setting Up Your Studio

If you want to be businesslike you'll have to have some policies. Set up a schedule and try to keep it regular, especially with younger students. Although I have not used this myself, it seems that you could communicate with all your students via Facebook, or a similar social networking site, if you set up a page that can only be viewed by them and thus protect it from the open Internet. For older students in particular, this would be a perfect way to communicate.

Lesson:

If you teach at home, make it a professional environment.

You'll have to decide on lots of particulars, beginning with a cancellation and makeup policy. Check the area and see what the usual lesson fee is and decide on a payment schedule. All of this information should be prepared in a business-like format and given to each student (read: their parents) each year. If you teach band or orchestra instruments you can get your name around by contacting area band and orchestra directors. Introduce yourself and offer to work with their students for an hour or so in a master class format. Play for them and coach them as a group. You shouldn't charge anything unless the band director insists. This is PR work.

On the business side of things, there will be tax advantages to you if your studio qualifies as a home office by the Internal Revenue Service's definition. (See the tax section in this book.) If it does, you will be able to deduct many of your business-related expenses from your revenue. Of course you will have to keep accurate books but, once again, you can use your computer to set up a system that will keep accurate and thorough records of all of your studio expenses.

Once or twice a year, you can put on some sort of public event—a studio recital. This serves as motivation for your students and is also an excuse for getting them all together to hear each other play. It is also an opportunity for you to invite prospective students and their parents to attend. If your class is a little small the first year, you can always partner with another teacher and share expenses. But avoid the two-hour marathon event. Keep the playing to an hour maximum, then give them some punch and cookies!

Teaching at home can be rewarding both personally and financially, and it also has quality of life advantages for some. Making it as professional as possible will heighten your sense of accomplishment, as well as your brand. A good reference book is *Making Money Teaching Music* by David R. Newsam and Barbara Sprague Newsam. Look for more specific information in the bibliography section of this book.

Getting Grants

As musicians we have a source of revenue available to us that most other professions do not have. It's grant money. According to Ellen Liberatori in her book, *Guide to Getting Arts Grants* there are over 66,000 grant-making foundations in the U.S.[16] Some subsidize organizations such as music schools, orchestras and chamber groups, while others support individuals. For individuals it is possible to receive funding for special projects, like writing a piece for a performing group. Travel/study grants or fellowships that advance one's career are available, and artist residencies are also an option. Since foundations disperse money that is earned off of their investments, they experience ups and downs in their philanthropic ability. When the economy is booming and the stock market is up, they can fund more projects and add to their investment portfolios at the same time. And, conversely, in a down period they must be more frugal.

> **Lesson:**
>
> Grant money is available, but you have to go after it. It's an investment of time.

There is money out there, but it's your job to find it. This requires research to uncover funding sources whose mission fits with your background, experience and interests. However, there is one necessary step that you must do before you apply for a grant: get your portfolio together. This includes a résumé, bio, curriculum vitae and examples of your work—scores and recordings if you are a composer or recordings if you are a performer or are a member of an ensemble. A well put together portfolio will, of course, have all sorts of applications outside of the grant-writing process.

Your Résumé

A résumé is a one or two page document that summarizes your background and experience relative to a particular job for which you are applying. Your résumé and cover letter are what a potential employer will initially use to screen job applicants. For this reason you must spend some time and thought when you put your résumé together. Fortunately there is a considerable amount of literature readily available on the web to help point you in the right direction, so there is no need to go into tiny details here. The information we have on the Eastman School's Institute for Music Leadership website under the Office of Careers and Professional Development is specific for music and will be very helpful. Use our sample résumés as templates and plug your information in. Find useful information here: esm.rochester.edu/iml/careers/library.php.

Your Curriculum Vitae

A curriculum vitae (CV, vitae or just vita) is used mainly for academic positions, but grant applications might also call for one. They differ from a résumé in length and detail, though the two terms are frequently used interchangeably. Whereas résumés are brief, one or two pages, and provide the documentation of your background and experience for a particular job, a vita represents your life's work. A résumé or bio might mention something without documentation, but a vita has all the backup documentation included. For example, the education section would include, for each degree, the granting institution, the year earned and—for a bachelor's

> **Lesson:**
>
> Start your CV today and update it at the end of each year.

degree—your major and minor. The publication section would include, for each published article, the date of publication, the name of the periodical, the volume and number, then page numbers. Follow the same format for books. In other words—thoroughly document your work, so the reader may locate each item if he wants to follow up. Though there is no limitation on length for a CV, you should use common sense. I have seen some CVs that have listed literally every solo concert played. That's overkill and unnecessary. Just list your important career events, and update it on a regular basis. From a complete and accurate CV, you can easily craft a résumé when the situation calls for it.

Your Bio

In addition to your résumé you need something that is written in prose for concert programs and the like. You should keep it to one or two paragraphs. It isn't necessary to document everything as you would with a CV, and it will vary with the situation as to the amount and the type of information you include. The style of your biography must be a little more reader friendly than a résumé or a CV. Here is my own "short bio" as an example. Note that it covers the full range of my background and experience and is on the lengthy side. A document with this amount of detail would be appropriate if I were asked to be an outside reviewer for a tenure case, and they wanted to know my academic/administrative qualifications. On the other hand, if I needed something for a concert program in which I were a soloist, I would omit much of the reference to my academic and administrative experience. In the same manner, if I were a member of an ensemble, like a woodwind quintet and a bio for each player was requested, it would be much, much shorter.

> **Lesson:**
> Extract your résumé and bio from your more inclusive CV.

Ramon Ricker is Senior Associate Dean for Professional Studies, Director of the Institute for Music Leadership and Professor of Saxophone at the Eastman School of

Music in Rochester, New York. As a senior administrator at Eastman, Dr. Ricker has been instrumental in shaping Eastman's innovative Arts Leadership curriculum that offers courses on Entrepreneurship and Careers, Leadership and Administration, Performance, Contemporary Orchestral Issues and The Healthy Musician. A full-time Eastman faculty member since 1972, he was the first titled saxophone professor at the school. He is also Editor-in-Chief of Polyphonic .org, an Eastman-sponsored website for professional orchestra musicians. From 1989 to 1998, he served as Chair of the Department of Winds, Brass and Percussion, and from 2000 to 2001 chaired Jazz Studies and Contemporary Media, co-chairing the same from 2001 to 2002.

His association with the Rochester Philharmonic Orchestra first began as a clarinet soloist in 1972. In 1974 he won a position in the RPO as a member of the clarinet section, and continues to play in the orchestra today. He served on its Board of Directors from 1997 to 2005.

He frequently performs as a guest saxophone and clarinet soloist and clinician in high schools and colleges throughout Europe and North America, and his books on jazz improvisation and saxophone technique as well as many of his compositions are looked to as standards in the field, with more than 140,000 copies sold worldwide with translations in French and Japanese.

He has performed and contracted the music for hundreds of television and radio commercials and themes, including national accounts for ABC, NBC, HBO and Arts and Entertainment. As a composer and arranger, he has been honored by grants from the National Endowment for the Arts, New York State Council on the Arts, Creative Artist Public Service, Meet the Composer and ASCAP. His arrangements have been commissioned by the Rochester Philharmonic and the American, Atlanta, Cincinnati and

North Carolina Symphonies, with works published by Advance Music (Germany), Alphonse Leduc (Paris), ATN (Tokyo), Alfred (USA) and Jamey Aebersold (USA).

A Cautionary Word about Résumé Padding

A very disturbing issue surrounding résumés is that some persons seem to feel the need to embellish, pump-up, inflate and down right lie about their background and experience. It seems crazy to me in the age of the Internet, in which a plethora of information on individuals is available almost instantly, but nonetheless it's done. Knowing that, most who deal with résumés on a fairly regular basis read them with a certain amount of skepticism. "Why did this person say he was nominated for a Grammy but didn't list the piece or the title of the CD?"

> **Lesson:**
>
> Don't pad, inflate, or stretch the truth on your résumé. Be honest.

Be aware that bold-faced lying is grounds for dismissal. In 2006 David Edmondson, the former CEO of Radio Shack, resigned after it was discovered that he claimed two degrees from a school he attended for only two semesters. And higher education is not exempt. In 2007 the Massachusetts Institute of Technology (MIT) Dean of Admissions was fired for claiming both a bachelor's and master's degree on her résumé, when in fact, she had earned neither. My advice is definitely do not lie. Be utterly honest.

Another bit of advice—don't inflate. It is quite common to list teachers with whom you have studied, but the inclusion of master classes is virtually worthless unless you actually played for and were coached by the artist teacher. If, on a résumé, I see "master classes with Yo-Yo Ma, Lynn Harrell and Steve Doane" it means nothing to me. Did you actually play and were coached or were you simply in the same room as this person as you observed the class for one hour? If they coached you, say it. Another thing—forget the inclusions in *Who's Who*. They don't mean anything at all. *Who's Who* sounds impressive, but in reality, they are vanity publications that make their money selling copies to the persons in the book.

Further, if you are a jazz musician, you can delete the list of famous artists with whom you have played if it was a one off. Playing one tune at a jam session or on the same stage with a famous artist in a school concert isn't that noteworthy. If you are a commercial or show player, you don't have to include all the acts that you have played. In reality practically every horn player in the country, of a certain age, has played in the backup band for the Temptations or the Four Tops.

As your career develops keep your CV up to date and delete items that are not that significant now. I was principal clarinet in the Colorado All-State Orchestra in my senior year of high school—a big deal to me then, but now—not so much. One way to rise above those who inflate their résumé is to offer more specifics on yours. For example, on paper a person who has played one rehearsal or one concert with an orchestra can appear the same as a person who has actually won an audition and has been given a contract or put on the sub-list. So, set yourself apart by giving some dates. On my own CV I specifically say recorded and toured with Buddy Rich and Chuck Mangione, instead of "played with." Again, by thoroughly documenting your accomplishments, the reader is able to follow up if he chooses to do so.

One More Preliminary

To get grant money you must have a track record. You probably won't be able to get funding to write a piece for orchestra unless you already have composed some large-scale works. If you are looking for support for an ensemble, the funders will want to know that you are already a bona-fide group that has been together for a period of time and has given concerts. I have seen some grant applications where, in order to apply, a specific number of concerts within a certain time period is specified. If you want to study abroad, you may be required to demonstrate some ability to speak the language of that country. If you are still in school there will be scholarships available to you, but money to fund compositions, tours or other projects might not be available until you are out of school.

So–Get Started Now

Get your CV up to date and keep it that way. If you get in the habit of periodically revising it, you won't overlook anything. The end of the year is a good time to do this. On New Year's Day get out your datebook, Blackberry or iPhone and review the year. Simply make note of relevant activities on your computer. With your biographic information in good shape, and good examples of your work well organized, the grant application process will go much quicker.

Where's the Money?

Presumably you have an idea or project already in mind. You want to study abroad, or you want to write a large-scale orchestra piece and get it performed, or get some funding for your string quartet to commission a new work.

> **Lesson:**
> Finding grants that fit what you do requires research.

Your job is to find a funder who supports the kind of project you have in mind, and once found, you must demonstrate that you have the background, experience and achievement in that field to be competitive among the pool of applicants. You can start by going to the library or looking online at three sources:

Foundation Grants to Individuals
  foundationcenter.org/findfunders/fundingsources/gtio.html

Foundation Directory Online
  fconline.foundationcenter.org/

National Directory of Corporate Giving.
  foundationcenter.org/marketplace/catalog/product_directory.jhtml ?id=prod10009

At the library there won't be a charge, but if you want to access these online you will have to pay a subscription fee or buy the publication. These three sources are important in your research. But there is also information available to you at no charge.

I just searched "music grants for individuals." Not everything that came up was relevant, but nevertheless there was some good information to get started. An interesting one that was right near the top was Michigan State University Libraries. They have an annotated list of foundations' websites, databases and books that offer funding for music, and there is no charge for this information! Find it here, staff.lib.msu.edu/harris23/grants/3music.htm

Other sources to investigate are:

The National Endowment for the Arts
    arts.endow.gov/grants/apply/Music.html

State, Regional, and Jurisdictional Art Agencies
    nea.gov/partner/state/SAA_RAO_list.html

Do searches of these topics:

- grants for nonprofit organizations
- grants for musicians
- grants for performing arts
- music grants and scholarships
- musician fellowships grants
- music travel study grants

You will have to sift your way through the entries, but this is an investment of your time. You can also do research by keeping your eyes and ears open. If you are in school, check out the bulletin boards around the composition department and the careers office; and talk to your friends about funding opportunities.

Most musicians who have at least a passing interest in finding grant money have heard of Fulbright and Guggenheim. These are prestigious awards. Lots of musicians apply for them and they are difficult to get. But in addition to the large more well-known foundations, there are a host of smaller ones whose mission is to fund a much more narrow segment of the population. In the early 1990s one of my saxophone students decided that after graduation with her bachelor's degree, she wanted to study in Paris with Jean-Michel Goury. She applied for a Fulbright, but applications to France are numerous and highly competitive. She didn't get it. However, she did do her homework. While applying for the Fulbright application (and without the aid of the Internet), she researched and found three other funding sources for which she would qualify. She figured she had already done the heavy lifting with the Fulbright application and that she would look for other possibilities for backup. The grants she found were quite specific, not well publicized and had far fewer applicants. Through a conversation with a friend, whom she would marry several years later, she was made aware of the Frank Huntington Beebe Fund for Musicians, whose purpose is to fund overseas study. She also uncovered the Harriet Hale Woolley Scholarship at the *Fondation des Etais-Unis,* which was specific in providing room and board at the *Fondation.* That was perfect. She had a place to stay. The third funding source was from the local chapter of Phi Beta Kappa at the University of Rochester. It was specific for education and study in Europe. The three awards together gave her much more money than a Fulbright, and she was able to stay in Paris for two years.

> **Lesson:**
> Once your application materials are assembled, apply for more than one grant.

Writing the Application

Follow the application guidelines and rules to the letter. Make sure they fund the type of project you are proposing. Spend some time crafting your project statement. It has to be convincing. Remember there are others applying for this same money along with you. Your idea has to be a good one and you have to sell it to the funders. They have to believe that you can do what you propose to do. Do your budget research. If your proposal involves other people or organizations—i.e., if you will perform your new composition at several venues around the city—include supporting documentation from the venues. Make sure you fill out all forms completely and include everything in the packet. Make the deadline. Grant deadlines are usually hard and fast, and the unfortunate late entry is summarily discarded. **Do not be late.**

I have been on grant review committees and they can be grueling. Many applications are immediately discarded because they haven't followed directions. Put yourself in the place of the adjudicators. They may spend an eight-hour day reviewing proposals and listening to music. They can get very weary. You will have to stand out and grab their attention, because they will spend only a couple of minutes listening before they make the first cut. (In reality it is probably the second cut. The first cut was most likely made by the foundation staff who have already thrown out the applications that didn't follow the rules.) Your supporting recordings should

> **Lesson:**
>
> Follow the grant application guidelines and rules to the letter.

be "hot." Not every piece when played from the beginning is impressive. If that is the case with one of your examples, you could say, "If time is a concern please listen from 15:30 to 17:45, measure numbers 246–392. Find tabs in the score that correspond to that section." This makes the adjudicators' job easier. Lead them to what you want them to hear. Remember, it's a competition and definitely not a done deal. For more grant application tips read "Know How to Get Lucky" in Chapter 10.

Being awarded a grant can add credibility to you as a musician. Someone, other than your mother, has said that they want to give you money to do a project, and they will give it to you because they feel it is worthwhile. They think doing so will help humankind in some way or other—bring joy, touch or inspire those with whom you will share your artistry. That's a lofty statement, but why else would anyone give you money to do something that you would do anyway?

Using the Web (Okay, you know about this one)

When I graduated from college an engineer friend of mine who was also graduating told me he was going to go to work for RCA. (It's funny how one remembers these isolated incidents from the past.) RCA was a major electronics company in its day, and he was going to be involved with computers. He explained to me something about computers working with 0s and 1s, and punch cards that were used to input data. I also knew that they were very large and took up a lot of space. That was in the mid-sixties, and much has changed since then. It is definitely an understatement to say that computers, the Internet and the World Wide Web have changed the way musicians do business!

Electronics—with its synthesizers, samplers, drum machines and sequencing—has surpassed the piano as the composer's most valuable tool. Music engraving programs now make the all-night part-copying session a thing of the past. The Internet and its search engines save us valuable time in research. We can get answers to just about anything in a matter of seconds. And if my German publisher sends me some music to edit, I can do it and get it back to her the same day. Social networks like Facebook, MySpace, LinkedIn and Twitter keep us connected and expand our reach if we want to use them for commercial purposes. We can easily get the word out when we want to promote a concert, and our personal websites provide a place for us to offer our wares for sale. Recently, I was considering the clarinet part on Stravinsky's *Ebony Concerto* that I would be playing soon in a concert in Rochester. I hadn't heard it in a while, and I wanted to see how much I would have to practice in order to sound decent on it. Ten years ago I would have gone to the library. But I found it on YouTube in probably less than ten seconds. If you are old enough to remember this, think back to when telephone answering machines first came on the scene. It was very annoying to have to leave a message. Nowadays if we make a

Lesson:

Move ahead with the times. Don't get stuck in the past. Embrace technology.

call and no answering machine picks up we're bugged! But who makes telephone calls anyway? I do all my contracting of musicians through email. Maybe younger people take this kind of information at your fingertips for granted, but it still amazes me. It's like we're on a moving train and it's accelerating!

The point of this cursory look at these technological advances is to remind you to embrace the future—technology in this instance—and change. Stay current with the latest Lego kits, and adapt or become irrelevant.

Royalties–Copyrights, Rights, Patents and Trademarks

Royalties are a good thing, and you, as a musician, have a better chance of receiving them than the average professional person. The basic concept is that if you create something, it is yours, and you have the right to be compensated if others use it. This right was provided for by the authors of the United States Constitution, and it empowers Congress in Article 1, Section 8, Clause 8, "To promote the Progress of Science and the useful Arts, by securing for limited Times to Authors and Inventors the exclusive Right to their respective Writings and Discoveries." This is the so-called Copyright and Patent Clause.

Lesson:

Royalties–Do something once. Get paid for it many times. Not a bad concept.

Without royalties a musician is like a barber. A barber cuts someone's hair and gets paid for it. The more haircuts he gives the more money he makes, but his financial condition is limited by the number of haircuts he can do. On the surface it's the same for musicians. We play a gig. We get money. The more gigs—the more money. With royalties, however, the balance changes: we can do something once and be repaid for it many times over. It's like planting a fruit tree. We put it in the ground and each year it pays us again by bearing fruit. For musicians there are several different ways we can receive royalties—print rights, mechanical rights, performance rights and synch rights. We'll discuss each of these, but first we have to talk about copyright.

Copyright

Everything you need to know about copyright can be found at copyright.gov, the official site of the U.S. Copyright Office. The site offers useful circulars, brochures, factsheets, reports and studies. You can also check on the status of proposed rule changes and amendments. If you are real hard-core you can download, at no charge, the official, "Copyright Law of the United States and Related Laws Contained in Title 17 of the United States Code, 2007," or purchase it for $29.50. It's 327 pages of tough reading, but you can find more user-friendly circulars on the site that will give you essentially the same information. Obviously, there are lawyers who specialize in copyright law, but I'm not in that group. What I will give you here are some basics that will help you protect what you create—your intellectual property.

Patents protect inventions or things, while trademarks protect names, words, logos, designs, etc. Copyright, on the other hand, is used to protect the following categories:

- literary works
- musical works, including any accompanying words
- dramatic works, including any accompanying music
- pantomimes and choreographic works
- pictorial, graphic and sculptural works
- motion pictures and other audiovisual works
- sound recordings
- architectural works

If you compose a piece today it will be protected for the duration of your life plus 70 years. Some things relevant to musicians that are not copyrightable are ideas, procedures, titles of songs, slogans and chord progressions.

As the owner of your creation you receive the following exclusive rights, which you may also authorize others to do:

- To reproduce the work in copies or phonorecords
- To prepare derivative works based upon the work

- To distribute copies or phonorecords of the work to the public by sale or other transfer of ownership, or by rental, lease or lending
- To perform the work publicly, in the case of literary, musical, dramatic and choreographic works, pantomimes and motion pictures and other audiovisual works
- To display the work publicly, in the case of literary, musical, dramatic and choreographic works, pantomimes, and pictorial, graphic or sculptural works, including the individual images of a motion picture or other audiovisual work
- In the case of sound recordings, to perform the work publicly by means of a digital audio transmission

In very simple terms, if you compose original music or arrange works taken from the public domain, or author books, like this one that you are reading right now, you own it, and your creation is protected from the moment it is put in tangible form, i.e., written down. It is protected, but should there be an infringement on your work (read: someone tries to steal it) you may not prevail in court unless the work is registered with the Copyright Office.

> **Lesson:**
>
> Protect your work by registering it with the U.S. Copyright Office.

Though it is no longer required under copyright law, it is still a good idea to include the notice of copyright's three elements on your works. It informs the public that the work is protected, and as we just discussed in connection with registration, it adds credence to an infringement case should that ever become an issue. The three elements are the symbol © (the letter c enclosed by a circle, or copr. or copyright spelled out); the year of first creation; and your name or your company's name. (Example: © 2011 You, Inc.)

This has been a very perfunctory discussion. I didn't mention fair use, public domain, joint authorship or how to actually file for copyright. There are still about 326 pages in the copyright law remaining to cover! But, now you know where to go. When the time is right you can find out about these and a host of other topics by checking out the U.S. Copyright Office's website.

Print Rights

Over my lifetime in music, I have written many original compositions, created arrangements of public domain and copyrighted pieces, and authored instructional or "method" books for saxophonists and aspiring jazz improvisers. In most cases I entered into royalty agreements with my publishers by assigning or licensing my copyright to them. In turn they have manufactured and marketed my creations—published them. I gave them the exclusive right to distribute my work and, in return, they give me a royalty for each unit sold. The usual rate for royalties from printed music or music books is 10 percent of the retail price, but that is always open to negotiation. These are royalties from print.

The publisher sells my works to retail and online music stores at a discount of 40 to 60 percent depending on how good a customer they are (read: how much product they buy). For illustration purposes let's say that the retailer gets a 50 percent discount. After my 10 percent that leaves 40 percent for the publisher, who must pay out of that sum the cost of design, printing, marketing, storage, etc., of the book. As an author you should watch out for offers of 10 percent of wholesale or any royalty based on a percentage of the "net." The "net" is the amount of money remaining after expenses, as opposed to the "gross," which is the total amount of money received. Creative accountants (if so inclined) can charge all kinds of expenses against your creation, thereby reducing the "net."

Mechanical Rights

A mechanical license grants the rights to reproduce and distribute copyrighted musical compositions (songs), including uses on phonorecords (i.e., CDs, records, tapes, and certain digital configurations). When you think mechanical rights, think Harry Fox Agency (HFA). "HFA is the foremost mechanical licensing, collections, and distribution agency for U.S. music publishers. Established in 1927, it acts as an information source, clearinghouse and monitoring service for licensing musical copyrights. It continues today to license, collect, and distribute royalties on behalf of U.S. publishers that own and/or control the rights to musical compositions."[17] Simply stated, if you want to record and distribute a song that was written by someone else, or if your business requires the distribution of music that was written by others, you must obtain a mechanical license.

Mechanical rights apply to audio compositions that are delivered without live performers i.e., mechanically. The term originates from early piano roll music. Picture a turn of the century (1900) player piano with the roll played mechanically by a person pumping away on foot pedals instead of actually touching the keys. From that early beginning mechanicals have evolved to cover a wide-range of copyrighted material including CDs, tape recordings, music videos, ringtones, MIDI files, downloaded tracks and DVDs.

Though U.S. copyright law gives the copyright holder the exclusive right to use his or her music on any of the formats cited above, it also provides that **once a composition has been recorded, any other party can record the piece without obtaining permission from the copyright holder.** Here is the important part. **The entity using previously copyrighted material must pay the statutory compulsory rate.** So—if it has been recorded, you don't have to ask permission. You just pay the statutory rate to the Harry Fox Agency and everything is legal and on the up and up.

As of this writing the present statutory rate is:

9.10 cents for songs 5 minutes or less, *or* 1.75 cents per minute or fraction thereof over 5 minutes. For example:

> Songs 5:01 to 6:00 = 6 x $.0175 = $.105
> Songs 6:01 to 7:00 = 7 x $.0175 = $.1225 (and so on)

Let's say that you have a tune that someone else wants to record. If it has previously been recorded they simply go ahead and make their version of it, and send a check to Harry Fox for the statutory rate of

9.10 cents per song, times the number of units they sell or distribute. Harry Fox then sends the royalties to the publisher, and the publisher then divides the money 50/50 between the publisher and the composer.

It is possible for the composer to also be the publisher, which is typical with self-published or small independent labels, but the bigger labels will often require the composer to enter into a co-publishing agreement with them. They frequently ask for 50 percent of the publishing. They simply won't take on your recording unless they get a piece of the mechanicals. Now the royalty to the composer is down to 6.825¢ per song. For a new artist the record company might even try to drive a harder bargain by asking for 100 percent of the publishing.

You can see that there is some serious money involved with mechanical rights. If an album has 10 songs on it at 9.10 cents per song, the amount generated per album is $.91. I'll let you multiply that out by a million or two to see what a best selling CD would produce! But that's not all! Down the road there is even greater potential for royalties. If the song turns out to be a hit and others want to record it, those mechanicals will go to the composer and the publisher. Thirty years ago I did some work with Jerome Kern songs. The publisher gave me a printout of all the artists who had recorded the pieces in which I was interested. One of those tunes was "All the Things You Are." I did the math. It had been recorded more than 600 times, and that was 30 years ago! Let's be conservative and say that only 1,000 units were sold with each of those 600 versions. That equals 600,000 units. Multiply that by 9.1¢ and you have $5,460,000. That's a lot of money even with this conservative example.

Songs (including classical compositions) can generate substantial amounts of money over time, and publishers' catalogues can have tremendous monetary value. In a much-publicized event in 1984 the entire 4,000-song catalogue of Associated Television Corporation (ATV) was offered for sale. It included most of The Beatles songs, and Michael Jackson bought it (read: acquired the publishing rights) for $47.5 million beating out his then friend Paul McCartney. The two reportedly never spoke to each other again. But with the recent death of Jackson, it has been rumored that in 2009 he changed his will, leaving the Beatles rights to McCartney. The accuracy of that story will unfold very soon now. But regardless of this latest twist, and before you start feeling sorry for McCartney or the John Lennon estate, remember Jackson only acquired the publishing rights. The composing royalties still go to McCartney and the Lennon estate.

Performance Rights

In 1897 an amendment to the copyright law provided that any person performing a dramatic or musical composition without the consent of the copyright owner would be liable for damages and potential criminal misdemeanor charges.[18] Prior to this, copyright protection was limited to printed music. This amendment was obviously well-received by composers and publishers, but without a mechanism to collect royalties it was practically unenforceable, since it is obviously impossible for a copyright holder to be everyplace his or her music is performed. But Europe provided a model.

Nearly 50 years prior to the 1897 U.S. amendment, a society was created in France, in 1851, to license and collect royalties on non-dramatic public performances of its works. In the U.S., Giacomo Puccini (1858–1924) proved to be a catalyst. When, in 1910, he discovered that this country had no performance rights organizations, he began a conversation with his publisher that eventually resulted in the establishment of the American Society of Composers, Authors and Publishers (ASCAP) in 1914. Early members included Irving Berlin, Victor Herbert, Jerome Kern and John Philip Sousa, the most popular songwriters of the day.

In addition to ASCAP, two other performance rights organizations (PRO) are active in the United States. Recognizing that ASCAP had a virtual monopoly on performance rights,

Lesson:

In the U.S., composers and publishers receive royalties through ASCAP, SESAC and BMI.

Broadcast Music, Inc. (BMI) was established in 1940 by radio executives who decided to create their own PRO and therefore pay themselves performance royalties instead of ASCAP. A third player in the field is SESAC (Society for European Stage Authors and Composers). It is privately owned and is much smaller than the other two organizations, but as it says on its website it prides itself in its ability to create individual relationships with the composers and publishers it represents. Apparently its small size is attractive to some artists, since it is not without big names on it roster. Bob Dylan, Justin Timberlake, Beyonce, Garth Brooks, Eric Clapton and Luciano Pavarotti are all represented by them.

Individuals can only be a member of one PRO at a time and they can join as a writer (composer) and/or a publisher. Deciding which one to sign up with can be difficult, since the information they put forth is often not directly comparable to each other. Here is some information to get you started. But you'll have to do your own research from this point forward.

ASCAP—ASCAP is member owned. It is the largest of the three. There is an application processing fee of $25, but there are no annual dues. To become an ASCAP writer member, you must have written or co-written a musical composition or a song that has been:

- commercially recorded (CD, record, tape, etc.); or,
- performed publicly in any venue licensable by ASCAP (club, live concert, symphonic concert or recital venue, college or university, etc.); or,
- performed in any audio visual or electronic medium (film, television, radio, Internet, cable, pay-per-view, etc.); or,
- published and made available for sale or rental.

BMI—As stated on their website, "If you're a songwriter or composer and have written songs that have the potential to be used on radio, television, the Internet, in restaurants and or any of the thousands of other businesses that use music, you've come to the right place." There is no application fee, and as you can see the entry bar is very low.

SESAC—As stated on their website, "Unlike the other performing rights organizations, SESAC has a selective process by which to affiliate songwriters and publishers, resulting in affiliates who have personal relationships with the SESAC staff. The company's creative staff works with songwriters to develop and perfect their talents. SESAC takes pride in a roster based on quality rather than quantity. Submissions are reviewed by SESAC's Writer/Publisher Relations staff."

So we have these three PROs in the U.S. If you are a copyright holder how do you get your money? It's complicated. The royalties come from restaurants, casinos, nightclubs, concert halls, radio, and television stations—virtually any venue where music is played or broadcast. When you sign up with a PRO you give them permission to collect your performance royalties, but these agencies can't be everyplace music is played anymore than an individual can. Knowing that, ASCAP, for example, uses a system of blanket licenses. The blanket license basically says, "For this year go ahead and play all the music that we license. You don't have to fill out any forms. Use as much as you want and for that privilege we will charge you a yearly fee." This is called a blanket license, and ASCAP has more than 170 different licenses of this type. The fee is determined using weighting formulas that bring into consideration demographics, market size, ticket prices, seating of the room, number of hours music is played, etc. The cost of the license will vary according to the amount of music being played and people receiving it. The New York Philharmonic will pay ASCAP more than the Colorado Springs Symphony. A jazz club in Chicago will pay more than a restaurant in South Bend.

In addition to the blanket license, ASCAP also has field agents who monitor newspapers and radio noting when and where music is being played. New venues can expect a visit from ASCAP if music is being played there. ASCAP lawyers are understandably experts in this area of the law, and local bar owners are no match for them. Refusal to pay for a license can result in a lawsuit with penalties and legal fees much higher than the license itself.

To the uninitiated this can sound like a mob shakedown for having music in your establishment! Just remember, as stated earlier in this section of the book, the basic point is that the U.S. constitution provides that if you create a piece of music it is yours, and you have the right to be compensated if others use it.

Synchronization Rights

The term, "synchronization rights" had its genesis in the early days of film when music was first synchronized with movies. It is still used today and over time has been expanded to include a myriad of other audiovisual productions that have been invented since the "talkies." "If you are using a copyrighted piece of music (music owned by another) and if you are making a reproduction of that music in connection with the following, you must get permission to use the composition from the copyright owner:"[19]

- Commercials
- Karaoke
- Television Programs
- Motion Pictures
- Theatrical Productions
- Music Boxes
- Corporate Videos
- Samples
- CDs / Cassettes
- Adaptations
- Computer Software
- Parodies
- Printed Sheet Music
- Internet

Just listen to the music on television for one hour. There is a good chance that you will recognize a "standard tune" or two. Currently, I have been noticing a jewelry commercial on the air playing, "It Had To Be You," in the background. In order for the producer of that "jingle" (read: commercial) to use the music, he had to obtain a synch license.

That license allows for a new version to be used in conjunction with the visual, and it pays a royalty to the copyright holder of the tune, but if the producer uses a previously recorded version of the tune there is yet another piper to pay. Let's say a version by Josh Groban is out there (if you can believe that one), and that particular version is the one that the producer has to have. He can use it, but he must also obtain a Master Recording License from the copyright owner.

> **Lesson:**
>
> Making money
> while you sleep
> is a good thing.

In simple terms: create your new version of copyrighted material—get a Synch License. Use someone's version of copyrighted material—get a Master Recording License for the version of the song that you will use, *and* get a Synch License from the copyright owner of the tune.

Synch Licenses are negotiated directly with the copyright holder and their procurement is not something that a novice, or for that matter even an experienced non-lawyer type, should attempt on his or her own. There are lawyers and music companies that can do that for you, but you can do more preliminary legwork. You can search for publisher information using online databases such as:

- ascap.com
- bmi.com
- sesac.com
- loc.gov/copyright

Royalties are definitely a good thing. As my friends and I used to say, "You have to find ways to make money while you sleep."

Patents and Trademarks

Patents are granted for inventions. You design a new reed clipper and if you want to prevent others from using your special way that the clipper works, you patent it. U.S. patents are good only in the U.S., its territories and possessions. Its term is 20 years. There is expense involved since searches must be done to verify that your design has not been previously patented. You do not need to have a patent attorney, but unless you have a lot of free time, and feel like gambling that you will do it right, it is wise to hire one.

"A **trademark** is a word, phrase, symbol or design, or a combination of words, phrases, symbols or designs, that identifies and distinguishes the source of the goods of one party from those of others. A **servicemark** is the same as a trademark, except that it identifies and distinguishes the source of a service rather than a product."[20] The symbol used to indicate a trademark or servicemark is ®. TM and SM are used for trademarks and servicemarks when the application is pending.

There is an Eastman School jazz ensemble that consists of five saxophones and a rhythm section. Over the years the group has won several *DownBeat* (magazine) awards and has released one record and two CDs. In 1980 we came up with its name—Saxology. It's a good name and I felt we should trademark it, so we did. Sometime in the early 1990s my son-in-law told me he saw a Saxology recording in a record store in Washington, D.C. I thought that was a little odd, since our first record didn't have wide distribution. It was mainly just for us to sell at gigs. Upon closer examination we discovered that an English saxophone quartet was using the same name and had a recording out that was being sold in the U.S. I contacted our attorney and after some back and forth the U.K. group was prevented from using the name in the U.S. We were also prevented from touring the U.K. under the Saxology name.

CHAPTER 8

Four Mantras That Will Help You Save Money

Make Taxes Work For You

TAXES! SAVE YOU MONEY? Sure, you have to pay them, so you might as well try to pay as little as legally possible. Taxes are usually an unfavorable topic of discussion for people everywhere. We don't like them. We usually think they are too high. It pains us to pay them, and politicians always promise to lower them. But be that as it may, they are a necessary evil. Necessary, that is, if we want roads, schools, police and fire departments, libraries and countless social services programs. In this chapter I won't be debating whether they are too high, if we should have a flat tax or if government is too big or too small. I'm coming from the premise that taxes are a fact of life. So how do we musicians live with them and maximize the deductions that are legally available to us, which incidentally will lower our adjusted gross income and thereby lower the amount of money we give to Uncle Sam. This segment of the book is meant to offer general ideas and tips and should not be construed to be legal advice. There are many subtle nuances in tax preparation, and the tax code can be subject to different interpretations. Consult your tax preparer for expert advice. With that said . . .

In the U.S. we have what is called a progressive tax system, which means that the tax rate *progressively* moves higher as income increases. People who make more money are taxed at a higher rate. Below are the 2009 tax brackets for a single person. These figures refer to your adjusted gross income. (We'll get to that later.) They are also not relevant for long-term capital gains, since they are taxed at a lower rate.

10 percent on taxable income between $0 and $8,350

15 percent on taxable income between $8,350 and $33,950; plus $835

25 percent on taxable income between $33,950 and $82,250; plus $4,675

28 percent on taxable income between $82,250 and $171,550; plus $16,750

33 percent on taxable income between $171,550 and $372,950; plus $41,754

35 percent on taxable income over $372,950; plus $108,216

Governments use taxes to promote social or economic goals. If it is considered beneficial to have more solar power in use, then tax breaks or credits can be given to encourage citizens to convert to solar energy for their homes. If you own a home and are currently paying it off in installments, you can deduct the interest on your mortgage loan. That is an incentive by the government to encourage more home ownership.

Lesson:

Check your 1099s for accuracy. Errors tend to occur here with greater frequency than with W-2s.

Let's agree that we need a certain amount of taxes to promote a higher standard of living, but in the true American spirit we all strive to pay as little as possible to the government from our earnings. The sum total of all the money an individual earns is called the gross. It is reported by your employer to the Federal Government in the form of a wage and tax statement called a W-2, and a copy is sent to you each

January for the previous year's work. It shows wages earned and taxes taken out by your employer. In contrast, for self-employed income you receive a 1099-MISC form, but if you are a private music teacher, for example, you must keep track of your total income yourself. The person or entity who hires you as an independent contractor is required by law to send the 1099-MISC if he paid you $600 or more in the calendar year. Since you are not on his regular payroll, no taxes will be taken out, but nonetheless you will be responsible for them at tax time. It is a misconception that if you do not receive a 1099 and make less than $600 you don't have to report it. As a U.S. citizen, income from all sources is taxable regardless of the amount and where it is earned in the world. Here's a case in point.

A former student of mine took a cruise ship job right out of college. He worked on the ship the better part of a year. For some reason he didn't receive a 1099 from the employer, but the income was reported to the Internal Revenue Service. (My guess is that the cruise ship line had an old address for this person and though it was mailed, the form never got to him.) Anyway—my student thought there would be no tax due, since he was "at sea." Guess again, Sinbad. The IRS caught up to him and hit him for the tax due on his earnings plus interest and penalties! The amount was substantial and he had to make arrangements with the IRS to pay it back over time. In truth, he was lucky not to have been slapped with a fraud charge.

Lesson:

Where taxes are concerned, if it seems too good to be true, it probably is.

So, we all have our income reported to the IRS via W-2 and 1099 forms, with copies sent to us. Looking at the W-2 you will see in box 5, "Medicare wages and tips." The number found there is the gross—the total amount you made from that employer. If you contributed to a retirement account such as a 401K or 403b, that amount will be deducted from your gross (box 5) and the remainder will be shown in box 1 (wages, tips and other compensation). In the section on investments a few pages ahead, you will see that there are many benefits to reducing your gross income by contributing to a retirement account. You get to pay less taxes and the money in the account grows tax-free.

In order for you to pay less tax (your goal) you must get your total income down to a lower level. Claiming deductions does this. Some deductions, such as moving expenses, student loan interest, certain retirement plans, etc., directly reduce total income. These deductions are called "adjustments" and after subtracting them from total income, the result is **Adjusted Gross Income**. Other deductions, like contributions to charities, mortgage interest, loss from fire or theft and medical expenses in excess of 7.5 percent of your adjusted gross income are available to all tax filers, and are called **Itemized Deductions**. While all taxpayers may deduct non-reimbursed employee business expenses, musicians tend to have more expenses, many of which are unique to them. I will address these specific deductions for musicians in the next few pages.

Musical Instruments and Equipment

When you buy an instrument or equipment that has a useful life of longer than one year, you can depreciate it over the tax life of the item—usually seven years. This has the effect of spreading out the deduction over time. An alternate course would be to expense the purchase (deduct the price paid) of the instrument in one year using Section 179 of the IRS tax code. This provides an immediate and one-time write off of the item. Whether to expense the instrument or to depreciate it is a question for your tax advisor, since there are conditions that must be met for both. For example, the Section 179 expense cannot be greater than total earned income.

If you sell something for more than you paid for it, you have a capital gain, on which the IRS requires us to pay tax. The good news is that, at least for now, the capital gain tax is generally less than the taxes we pay on our income. But, let's say we bought a saxophone for $5,000, and over seven years we depreciate it down to zero. We decide to sell the instrument and we find that these instruments are in greater demand now than when they were new! They have actually *appreciated,* rather than *depreciated!* We are pleasantly surprised to find we can sell the sax for $7,000, which we quickly do. But as we walk away, counting our $2,000 profit, a thought stops us cold. We don't just have a $2,000 capital gain on which to pay taxes. We have to add, into ordinary income, the total depreciated amount—$5,000. That results in a capital gain of $2,000, plus ordinary income (taxed at a higher rate) of $5,000. What's more, even if the instrument did *not* appreciate and we sold it for $2,000, we would have ordinary income of $2,000, since we depreciated it down to zero.

Here's another example of instrument appreciation. If you have old string instruments beware! In William T. Hunt's excellent article on Polyphonic.org he writes:

> In the past, the IRS has taken the position that old string instruments are antiques that appreciate in value and therefore are not depreciable. There have been several court cases involving this issue.
>
> The most recent rulings have maintained that antique instruments used in a trade or business are subject to the same wear and tear as any other property used in a trade or business, and therefore are deductible. Based on these court cases it appears, at least for the present, that all musical instruments, including old string instruments, are deductible as long as they are actually used in a trade or business (i.e., having the instrument in a display case or hanging on a wall would not satisfy this requirement). However, the IRS disagrees with these decisions and may still disallow the deduction outside of the judicial circuits where the cases were decided.[21]

This discussion of depreciation has been from 40,000 feet. When you get down to street level there is much more to learn and absorb. For example, there are several methods of calculating depreciation. In my opinion, that is why you seek the advice of a tax professional.

Office in Home

In our homes or apartments, musicians all have a room in which they practice or teach, but for that room to be considered a home office and deducted on our taxes, it must meet certain requirements established by the IRS. For example, that part of your home must be used *regularly and exclusively*:

- as your principal place of business for any trade or business; and
- as a place to meet or deal with your patients, clients or customers in the normal course of your trade or business; and
- in the case of an employee, the home office must be for the convenience of the employer.

If the room is used for any other purpose like watching television, playing pool or entertaining, it will be disallowed. The space must be used for business purposes only.

Lesson:

An office in your home will help with taxes, but make sure it qualifies.

For the musician who has a space that is regularly and exclusively used for teaching there is little question. It qualifies as a home office. But for a performing musician who uses the space as a practice room there has been some back and forth—yes, no, yes. At the present time musician's practice rooms do qualify as home offices. Again on polyphonic.org William T. Hunt writes an informative article detailing the back and forth history that musicians will find very relevant.[22]

A home office can be very beneficial to the musician. Calculate the square footage of the office then divide it by the total square footage of the home or apartment. That will give you the percentage of the home that is used for business. Let's say that 10 percent of your home is used as a home office. You can then write off 10 percent of your home expenses to your business. Things like:

- Mortgage interest
- Property taxes

- Casualty or theft losses
- Homeowners insurance
- Rent payments
- Repairs and maintenance
- Utilities

If you make a capital improvement to the office by painting it or putting down a new carpet, those expenses can be fully deducted.

Home offices are a good thing. Tax audits are a bad thing! Keep impeccable records and make sure your particular room qualifies as a home office. There are other subtleties beyond what we have discussed here, so consulting a tax professional is advised.

Travel, Meals and Entertainment

Be careful. It's easy to see that abuse can happen in this area. If you combine a vacation with business make sure to separate the expenses for the two. Travel expenses for your spouse is not allowed unless he or she is an employee, or an officer in your company. Meals are only deductible at 50 percent. Keep a travel journal and accurate records of meals, including the date, time, with whom and for what purpose.

Other Deductions

- Supplies—items such as drumsticks, reeds, strings, cables and office supplies
- Recording costs
- Accounting fees
- Lawyer fees (only business related or to produce income)
- Music books and CDs
- Subscriptions to trade magazines
- Internet access and email (subtract any personal use)
- Telephone—have a separate business line (Your primary phone line is not deductible, but features may be, like call waiting, messaging, etc.)

- Lessons and coachings
- Education expenses—things that will further your career
- Advertising
- Website
- Instrument repair
- The list goes on and on

Closing Tax Thoughts

It goes without saying that you must keep good records. In addition, keep a journal. Record your appointments not only to keep you organized and on schedule, but also to provide a record of your business activities.

Lesson:

Separate your business and personal finances, and keep good records.

Now the hard part: keep all receipts. But just don't throw them in a drawer or envelope. Get an expandable file and label each pocket with categories such as: income, supplies, postage, instrument repair, etc. As bills and receipts come in throughout the year, pop them in the file in the appropriate section. At tax time you will be way ahead of the game.

Separate your business and personal functions—separate checking and credit card accounts. Consider formalizing your business. Get a DBA. (That will be covered in just a few pages.) Remember, the name of the game is lowering your adjusted gross income through legitimate tax deductions. Know what you can deduct, then use a professional to prepare your return. If you find one who is familiar with musicians, you will be repaid many times over by having professional expertise and advice. And by the way, their fee is deductable!

Lawyers Are Your Friends

At some point in our lives most of us will need a lawyer. I know there are hundreds of jokes floating around out there that question their character (I've told a few myself), but my experience with them has always been positive. If we buy a house we will need a lawyer, or if we are charged with a crime we will definitely need one! But as musicians, especially if we write, publish or record music we will need legal advice at some point. Used properly they can save you much time, money and aggravation. But the first thing you have to get over is the fact that they will charge you money for their expertise. Students frequently come to me asking for advice on contracts that they have been given to sign. They almost always ask me if they will need an attorney and, if so, how much will it cost. I can tell in their voice that they don't want to use a lawyer—like it's going to be a waste of money, or something. If you sign a contract and you don't fully understand

> **Lesson:**
> Don't "do it yourself" when it comes to legal issues. Lawyers are your friends.

what is in it, you could be making a big mistake that could impact you for many years to come. We are all aware of enterprises such as, "Divorce Yourself" or "Set Up Your Own Corporation." Maybe they work and are perfectly legal, but if for some reason the legality of an action is ever challenged, I would feel much more confident if my contract had been prepared and filed by an attorney, rather than by myself as a "do it yourself" project. Don't be cheap. Do it right. After all it will be deductible on your taxes!

When do you need a lawyer?

If you are asked to sign something, like a recording or a publishing contract, or a contract with a personal or business manager or agent, you should have legal advice. If you have the sense that a wrong move could be costly in time or money, or you don't completely understand the language or meaning in the contract, you need a lawyer. If the other side has a lawyer you definitely need one! Don't believe the line, "It's just a standard contract." "Standard contracts" that are written by the other side are biased toward the party who writes them.

How to find a good lawyer

When I teach my Entrepreneurship in Music class at Eastman, I always have a lawyer as a guest speaker. Over the years I have had three attorneys from the firm of Nixon Peabody, LLP—John Partigan, Peter Durant and Michael Cooney. Here is what I've learned.

There are good lawyers and bad lawyers just like there are good and bad musicians. They also specialize just like we do, so a divorce lawyer may not be the best person to look over the terms of a recording contract. A bad lawyer or one not fully familiar with the area of the law where you need assistance can cost you money in the long run. Some lawyers may be cheaper, but they might have to spend more time doing research than attorneys who have specific knowledge right off the top of their heads. In a worst-case scenario, bad lawyers may just give you bad advice.

So how do we find a good lawyer? Start by asking around. Friends, teachers and other musicians are a good place to begin. You can also call the bar association or a large law firm and ask for recommendations. If you go the large firm route they will have a cadre of attorneys each specializing in different aspects of the law. If you need to set up a sole proprietorship or corporation, there are many who can help you, but if you want something trademarked or patented, you will need a person who specializes in that. There are entertainment lawyers as well. At the outset, however, unless a record company is courting you, you probably don't need a New York or Los Angeles entertainment lawyer.

In choosing an attorney it is perfectly normal and usual to interview them. It can be a short meeting in their offices, or better yet you can meet them for lunch. This is a "get to know you meeting." The relationship on which you are embarking has to be good and feel right. In this first meeting, a good lawyer will tell you if you need legal services and whether their skill set is right for the job.

Lesson:

Lawyers are paid for their time. When you deal with them be prepared and get to the point.

As an example, let's say you have decided to set up a Subchapter S corporation. (You'll learn what that is in a couple of pages.) You've done your homework and that is what you think is best for you. At the lunch the lawyer will ask you questions about your business, e.g., its current status and your future business plans. A good lawyer will also be interviewing you, getting a sense of whether you are level-headed, have the ability to pay and won't turn out to be a high-maintenance pain in the you know what! Just in this initial conversation, you may discover that you really don't need a sub S, but an LLC would be better. You'll also discuss legal fees. They could be straight time (hourly), or a fixed fee for this particular job (hourly rate but not to exceed a certain amount). You should ask for an estimate. My experience has been that my attorney's estimates have been very close if not spot on, but the work I have had done has been very straightforward.

There is another type of payment that is sometimes used, called a contingency fee. With this arrangement the attorney is paid *contingent* upon winning the case, and legal fees are limited to 1/3 of the settlement. This fee structure is often used for lawsuits where personal injury has occurred and large sums of money are at stake.

Once you have selected an attorney, it's your job to be prepared for consultations. He or she is "on the clock" when you call. The meter is running, so get to the point. Be clear in your thinking and what you are asking him or her to do. If the two of you are looking over a contract, skip over the things you already understand. Ask your lawyer to review the entire document, but to explain points 7 and 15, if those are the ones that are unclear to you. In addition to preparing legal documents on your behalf, use him or her to teach you, explain, advise and if necessary to be your advocate, negotiator and—if worse comes to worst—scapegoat.

Create a Business

When you first enter the world of the professional musician, you may not be that busy at the outset. Your business is you, and like any other business you have to build it. The upside is that you will have much more time to practice than when you are older and more established. In these early years you may have to take a "day-gig" to support yourself. If that is the case, hopefully you will find something with flexible hours that will allow you to take a playing job if one arises. But, if you hang in there, meet people and get your name around, work will begin to pick up for you.

In the beginning you will probably play many cash paying gigs. We all know (read: musicians and the Internal Revenue Service) that there

is a lot of musician's work that has the potential to be paid "under the table." People who hire you are supposed to send you a tax form: either a W-2 if you are an employee or a 1099 if you are an independent contractor and have made $600 or more that year. Whether they do or not, your responsibility is to report your income and pay the taxes on it. But with that comes a bit of a sting. In some ways I suppose it can feel good to receive money that is not taxed, but like most things, that can have a downside, as well. Aside from being illegal, risking and carrying with it the possibility of nasty problems with the IRS, you may, some day, want to get married, establish credit, send your kids to college or buy a house. In order to qualify for a mortgage you have to show that you make enough money to pay for it. You generally will have to show the bank two to three years of tax returns, especially if you are a freelancer. Without a solid record of responsible tax payment, your future plans could be compromised.

As time goes on, and you start getting your own gigs, you will most likely have to pay the other musicians. If you mix this money that is coming in and going out with your personal finances, you will soon have a financial mess on your hands. It's not absolutely necessary, but you might decide to formally set up a business to alleviate this problem.

Even if you don't want to form a company, you can take steps to do a couple of simple things to make your life easier at tax time.

The first thing you can do is to separate your business and personal finances. Presuming you already have a checking account, just open a second account in your name, but use it only for business. You can do the same with a second credit card. Get one and use it only for business. As you accumulate funds you will want to have a separate account for savings, like a money market account. By doing these simple things, there will be just one place your business money goes in to and comes out from. You will be able to keep track of it better, and profit or loss will go on Schedule C of your federal tax form. Remember the true American spirit of striving to pay as little taxes as possible to the government? You'd be surprised how much your business expenses can reduce your taxable earnings. Look back at the section on taxes. Musicians usually have many deductions that they can claim at tax time, but not if they don't keep good records.

Now, let's say a few years go by, and you want to be a little more professional. You want to make your clients feel like they are dealing with someone who is solid, for real, professional, and together. At this point you might consider officially forming a company. If you decide to do this, do your homework. Take what follows below as a starting point, but read up and do your own research. In my own case I have had two partnerships with my wife, and I currently have a Subchapter S corporation. In all cases I spoke with a lawyer first to help guide me. I suggest that you do the same when considering anything other than a sole proprietorship. (See below.)

Another point to consider, before you create a company, is that you should be in business to make money. You can't go to the trouble to set something up, throw a lot of expenses at it and show no income. It has to be a business and not a hobby. If your "business" doesn't show a profit in at least three out of five years, the IRS may consider it a hobby, and your likelihood of an audit is increased. If this is a bona-fide business, you will be able to deduct expenses against your income, but if this is just a hobby, *or the IRS determines it just a hobby,* your expenses will be limited up to the amount you earn from the hobby. I presume that most of you reading this book are serious about being musicians, so commit to your future and act like businessmen. Set up specific accounts so you can keep good books and records. Go one step further: get business cards and advertise.

Sole proprietorship—A business structure in which an individual and his or her company are considered a single entity for tax and liability purposes.[23]

This business entity is the simplest to set up, and if you are currently freelancing you already have one. If you want your company to have a name other than your own, for example, "Joe Brown Music," you must get a DBA (Doing Business As). You will not be able to work legally under the assumed name or get a business checking account unless you have the DBA, which is actually a simple process. First you go to the county clerk's office and research the name that you want to use. Obviously it has to be available, and not in use by someone else. After you have verified that it is available, you purchase the registration form, which in most counties is a nominal cost (between $3 and $5). You fill it out, pay a $30 filing fee and file it with the county clerk. You're done. However, you may want to obtain an Employer Identification Number (EIN), especially if others will be working for you. This will prevent your social security number from going to others.

Lesson:

You probably already have a sole proprietorship and don't know it.

A word of advice before you seal the deal: it pays to think ahead when you decide on a company name. If you think you will be composing and arranging music, and will eventually be joining ASCAP, BMI or SESAC under your company's name, you should search the name in their databases. I made this mistake with my first company, which I called Black Swan Music. Eventually I wanted to join ASCAP as a publisher, but my company name was too close to an existing one, and my application was denied. I had to dissolve Black Swan Music and form an entirely new company.

A sole proprietorship is simple and easy. It's a one man or woman operation. It's all up to you. Your income and business deductions are given on Schedule C of the federal tax return form 1040. And you usually don't need a lawyer to set it up. Now you know the upside. The downside is that you are personally liable for any debts that might be incurred. This means that if your business defaults on a debt, the creditor can come after your house or other possessions. That's definitely not a good thing, but we'll talk about that later. For now, we'll talk about a few more ways to set up your business.

Partnerships—A relationship of two or more entities conducting business for mutual benefit.[24]

This business structure is one step up from a sole proprietorship. There are two different forms—general partnership and limited partnership. In a **general partnership** the parties are, for all intents and purposes, co-owners. No formal registration is required, so if you have a chamber group or band you may already have a partnership and don't know it! This is not a good thing, since similar to a sole proprietorship, each party in a general partnership is personally liable for the debts of the partnership. This means that if the cellist in your string quartet books a concert, but doesn't give everyone complete

> **Lesson:**
>
> If you play in a chamber group or band you may have a partnership and don't know it.

information and your group does not show up on the agreed date, the promoter may sue you. It doesn't matter that the three "innocent" parties didn't even know about the date. The cellist was dealing with the promoter on behalf of the group and everyone in the group (read: the partnership) is personally liable. It can get worse. Let's say the other three members are students and essentially have no money, but you are older and have a bank account with some money in it. You may end up paying the entire debt!

You can see that a partnership is more risky than a sole proprietorship. With a sole proprietorship you only have to worry about yourself. If you make a mistake in judgment you suffer the consequences, but in a partnership you have the others to worry about, and a misstep by one of them could (read: will) affect you.

If you have a chamber group and you start getting serious about it, you should consider getting things down in writing and filing some legal papers. A lawyer can help here. Among other things, you will want to clearly state how profits will be split, how capital will be contributed, each individual's duties, how a person can be dismissed from the group, how replacements are chosen and how the group's assets are divided upon its termination.

Within a **limited partnership** there are two kinds of partners—general and limited. The general partner (or partners) makes all decisions and manages the company. A limited partner (or partners) contributes capital to the company, but has no input into the decision-making process of the entity. However, in addition to his limited decision-making, his financial risk is limited as well to the amount of capital he has contributed to the company. This protects the limited partner from risking personal assets. I have personally never come across a musician who had a limited partnership for his/her music business, but I suppose it could be a viable option if a rich uncle wanted to help you out and not put his personal assets in jeopardy. In both partnership forms you need to file a DBA.

C Corporation—A business, which is a completely separate entity from its owners, unlike a partnership.[25]

Unlike a sole proprietorship or partnership that can be thought of as an extension or part of you, a corporation is a separate tax entity. When a corporation is formed it puts a barrier between you and your business. Consequently, if your business fails or you incur an unpayable debt, your creditors cannot come after your personal assets. A corporation continues into perpetuity after you leave or die, and you can raise capital by selling stock in the company. It is slightly more expensive to operate than non-incorporated entities. Depending on the state in which your company is incorporated, there may be state corporate tax due. There is also the issue of double taxation—taxed first at the corporate level then again on the shareholder level when shareholders receive earnings in the form of dividends. In reality this double taxation rarely happens with musicians. Since they typically have a corporation of a small number of people—perhaps themselves and a spouse—they usually pay themselves a salary or bonus and not dividends. Salaries and bonuses are normal business expenses and reduce corporate income,

> **Lesson:**
>
> A corporation puts a barrier between your personal and business assets.

but dividends do not. But a better way for most musicians to have their personal assets protected and separate from their business is to set up a **Subchapter S corporation.**

Subchapter S Corporation[26]—A form of corporation, allowed by the IRS for most companies with 100 or fewer shareholders, which enables the company to enjoy the benefits of incorporation but be taxed as if it were a partnership.

The older S Corporation business entity has largely been replaced by the more recent LLC, but it nevertheless still offers a good solution to the needs of some musicians. It provides for the limited liability of a corporation while the profits are "passed through" and reported on Schedule E of the federal tax form 1040. In the state of New York there is a corporate tax of $25–$4,500, depending on your income. Other states may impose similar taxes, so you'll have to look into that on your own if you decide to form a Subchapter S and don't reside in New York. There are other rules in order to qualify. Each shareholder must be a U.S. citizen or resident and there can be no more than 100 shareholders.

Limited Liability Company (LLC)—A type of company, authorized only in certain states, whose owners and managers receive the limited liability and (usually) tax benefits of an S Corporation without having to conform to the S Corporation restrictions.[27]

As stated previously, the LLC has largely replaced the Subchapter S as a preferred entity that offers protection for personal assets and provides favorable tax treatment for individuals by passing through profits to the owners to be reported on their personal tax return.

Limited Liability Partnership (LLP)—Another name for a Limited Liability Company. It is often used by professional associations. The partner's or investor's liability is limited to the amount he or she has invested in the company.[28]

This is essentially a general partnership but each partner is protected from the actions of the other partners. Their liability is limited.

Not-for-Profit Organization—An incorporated organization, which exists for educational or charitable reasons, and from which its shareholders or trustees do not benefit financially, also called non-profit organization.[29]

These organizations are board controlled. There are no owners, but don't be misled by the name. They can pay salaries and deduct expenses as long as these salaries and expenses are "reasonable." In addition, they can make a profit. They are also exempt from taxation. One must apply for tax-exempt status, and by its nature these entities may be under more scrutiny. Consequently good records and squeaky-clean adherence to the rules is a must.

> **Lesson:**
>
> Not-for-profit status can be suitable for musical groups, if they have an educational mission.

Many music ensembles consider this entity when they decide to formalize their relationship. And this may make sense for a group that intends to primarily perform outreach concerts.

The tax-exempt status sounds appealing and the educational fit is good. They may also have the perception that they will be looked upon more favorably when applying for grants. In spite of these compelling attributes, most ensembles will do more than community concerts, which makes the 501(c)(3) (tax exempt) status an unlikely fit for most.

Invest in Yourself, Invest in Your Future

You might be asking yourself, "What is this guy doing talking about financial planning in an entrepreneurial music book?" Well, in my interactions with young people through teaching, I have found that a high percentage of music students often have serious credit-card debt and no real idea about money in general, i.e., what they will do to earn it and how they will preserve it. Self-employed or largely self-employed people, in particular, need to be money wise. It is well beyond the scope of this book to discuss finances in depth. And I'll say right up front that I am by no means a financial expert. You must do your own research and chart your own financial path, but this chapter has some basics to get you started. We will begin the discussion with . . .

The Eighth Wonder of the World–Compound Interest

Systematic and regular saving combined with the compounding of interest can, over time, yield impressive results. Even if you are in your twenties and are looking at forty years until retirement, you should start saving for it now. The chart below demonstrates this well. From it you can see that if a person starts at age 25 and invests $25 each month, earning a 10 percent interest compounded monthly, the account will yield $158,102 at age 65. You can also see that if the start of savings is delayed, say until age 45, it will yield only $18,984 at 65, and to equal the person who started with $25 at age 25, it will take $200 a month at age 45! Of course inflation has to be accounted for, and one might also ask where can you get a 10 percent interest rate nowadays. Actually, since 1926 the stock market's average annual return on common stocks (taking into account both capital appreciation and dividends) has been over 10.3 percent.[30]

A quick way to calculate how long an investment will take to double is to use the **Rule of 72**. It's very simple, just divide 72 by the interest rate and the result is the number of years it will take for your money to double. For example, a 9 percent interest rate will double your money in 8 years (72 divided by 9 = 8). You can reverse it to find the interest rate necessary to double you money over a certain time period. The number 72 divided by years = interest rate. For example, 72 divided by 6 years would equal an interest rate of 12 percent. Remember, this calculation is without contributing any more money. It's just compound interest at work.

COMPOUND INTEREST EXAMPLE

PRINCIPAL AVAILABLE AT AGE 65
@ 10% INTEREST (COMPOUNDED MONTHLY)

STARTING AGE	MONTHLY INVESTMENT			
	$25	$50	$100	$200
25	$158,102	$316,204	$632,408	$1,264,816
30	$94,916	$189,832	$379,664	$759,328
35	$56,512	$113024	$226,049	$452,098
40	$33,171	$66,342	$132,683	$265,367
45	$18,984	$38,285	$75,937	$151,874

How to Save–Pay Yourself First

When you earn money it's a good idea to estimate what your monthly wage, whatever that amount may be, will buy. It's just common sense. You can't buy an airplane if you make $35,000 a year, but you might be able to afford a nice bike. Let's assume you make $35,000 a year, live in New York State, take the standard deduction and have one exemption—you. At 2008 rates, you will pay $7,676 in federal, state tax and Social Security (FICA) taxes. That will leave you with $27,324, ($35,000 minus $7,676), or $2,277 monthly take home pay ($27,324 divided by 12). You might have a credit card or two, but you have to be careful with them. You should live within your means.

From the monthly wage you can make a budget. List your expenses—housing, food, car, loans, insurance, etc.—all the things you have to pay for. (It will probably be a little depressing. There might not be much margin remaining for extras, but somehow it will work out.) On the expense side of the ledger pay yourself a fixed amount and put it in the bank. Even if it is just $10, do it. It doesn't have to be a large amount of money—just *save* something. If you do pay yourself first, the money is "spent" and hopefully you will forget about it. Out of sight—out of mind. But your money will begin working for you immediately, accruing interest at a compounded rate. Year by year, as you become better established, you can increase the monthly amount you pay yourself. Obviously, the more money you save, the more interest it will make for you. The main thing is to get in the habit of saving right from the start of your early working years. In the case of compound interest, old money is smarter than new money.

> **Lesson:**
>
> Get in a habit of saving money every month. You're investing in your future.

Money for Different Purposes

For musicians it is important to have the best instrument or instruments that you can afford. That should be a top priority, because it represents your livelihood. This may pose a problem if you play a string instrument, but don't give up on that. By doing some research, trading up, a little wheeling and dealing and maybe a loan from a relative, you can improve your lot. The good thing is that high-quality instruments generally keep a high-resale value, and in the case of string instruments they can appreciate and become very good long-term investments. You might be thinking, "How can I afford to buy an expensive instrument if I'm on a strict monthly savings plan?" I'm glad you asked!

I have found it beneficial to have two categories of saved money— short-term savings and long-term savings. Short-term savings are obviously for more immediate things that I want or need. A new instrument would fall into this category, as would money to purchase a house or a car. These are funds that I want to be readily available and not tied up for the long term. If my time horizon to make a major purchase is less than five years, I would be very careful about putting this money into stocks, because with the ups and downs of the market they might

> **Lesson:**
>
> Separate "saved money" into two categories: short term and long term.

have a dip in value just when I am hoping to use these funds to make a down payment on a house. Stocks are for the long haul. (You will read about some shorter-term alternatives a little later in this chapter.) By long-term savings I mean money for retirement. Remember the eighth wonder of the world!

A few years ago I was in New York City and had a Monday night free so I decided to go down to the Village and hear the Vanguard Band. I had a couple of friends playing in the group, so it was fun hanging with them on breaks. I got into a conversation with a friend from school who was in his early fifties, and he started bringing me up to date on his career. He was a little down. His Broadway show had just closed. The recording scene was starting to wane. He had a line on an adjunct position at a college in the tri-state area, but it fell through. It seems that even though he

> **Lesson:**
>
> Prepare for your financial future. Save for your retirement years and start early.

had lots of good playing experience, he hadn't done any real teaching, so another person got the job. He had started a family later in life and still had a couple of kids in elementary school. He said something to me that really hit home. "When I got out of school all I wanted to do was play, and now it looks like I'm going to have to."

The lesson for me that night was: prepare for the future. Think ahead. My friend could have taken steps to move his career from playing to more teaching, but that takes time and planning. Paying for your children's education also takes foresight. I have no idea whether my friend's finances were in good shape, but I am certain he was facing some hefty expenses. The point to remember is that it is better to act rather than react. A lot can happen 30 or 40 years into the future. You could have health issues. You could be divorced a couple of times. (That is definitely not recommended.) If a long-haul course is not charted early on, you will have to resort to damage control. Save for your retirement years and start early.

Pre-tax Saving

If you have bought into the idea that saving money is good, then you are really going to like putting away money before tax is taken out—pre-tax saving. The federal government wants its citizens to save for an independent retirement, and to encourage us to do that, there are certain incentives in the tax code. They have said, in effect, if you put $100 a month (for example) in an account (a 401k or 403b), you won't have to pay income tax on that right now. That $100 a month comes right off the top and lowers your total income. This is part of the calculation leading to adjusted gross income, and that is an important component of the amount on which your income tax obligation is calculated. Since it is a lower number you will owe less tax, and therefore pay less to federal and state governments at the end of the year.

> **Lesson:**
>
> Pre-tax saving is the most advantageous way to save money for retirement.

In addition, the money in the account can grow tax-free. However, it is important to remember that your tax obligation has only been deferred, not erased, and you will have to pay the tax on that $100 when your funds are withdrawn. But presumably that will be when you are retired and in a lower tax bracket. Of course there are some rules. You have to work for a company or organization that has one of these plans. There are limits to the amount you can contribute, and unless an exception is granted there is a penalty of 10 percent additional tax if you withdraw the money prior to age 59½. Following are three scenarios that demonstrate and compare the effects of pre-tax saving.

Effect of Reducing Your Gross Earnings with a 401k or 403b

For the three following examples, let's assume your taxable income is $50,000; Social Security taxes will remain the same in all examples, so for simplicity we will only consider Federal and New York State income taxes using 2008 tax rates. We will also assume that taxable income for Federal tax is the same as for New York State tax and that you are single.

CASE 1: You do no saving with a 401k or 403b

Taxable Income:	$50,000
Your Federal taxes:	$8,850
Your NY State tax:	$3,030
Total Tax due:	$11,880

The amount you make minus the tax is what you get in your paycheck.

	$50,000 (taxable income)
minus	$11,880 (taxes taken out)
equals	$38,120 (after taxes)

Divide $38,120 by 12 months and that gives you $3176.67 per month take-home pay.

CASE 2: Your income is the same as Case 1, but you invest 10% in a 401k or 403b

Case 1 Total Income:	$50,000
You invest pre-taxed dollars in a 401k or 403b:	$5,000 (10%)
Total taxable income is now lowered to:	$45,000
Your Federal taxes:	$7,600
Your NY State tax:	$2,687
Total Tax due:	$10,287

Again, the amount you make minus the tax is what you get in your paycheck.

	$45,000 (taxable income)
minus	$10,287 (taxes taken out)
equals	$34,713 (after taxes)

Divide $34,713 by 12 months and that gives you $2,892.75 per month take-home pay.

That's $283.92 less per month take-home pay than in Case 1, but $5,000 in the bank, and $1,593 less taxes paid at the end of the year.

CASE 3: Your income is the same as in Case 1, but you invest 20% in a 401k or 403b

Previous Taxable Income:	$50,000
You invest pre-taxed dollars in a 401k or 403b	$10,000 (20%)
Total taxable income is now lowered to	$40,000
Your Federal taxes:	$6,350
Your NY State tax:	$2,345
Total Tax due:	$8,695

Again, the amount you make minus the tax is what you get in your paycheck.

	$40,000 (taxable income)
minus	$8695 (taxes taken out)
equals	$31,305 (after taxes)

Divide $31,305 by 12 months and that gives you $2608.75 per month take-home pay.

That's $567.92 less per month take-home pay than Case 1, but $10,000 in the bank, and $3,185 less taxes paid at the end of the year.

The table below summarizes and provides for easier comparison.

	Taxable Income	Income after Retirement Contribution	Total Tax	Net Annual Income	Monthly Take-Home Pay	Annual Tax Saved	$ in the Bank at Year End
Invest $0	50,000	50,000	11,880	38,120	3,176.67	0.00	$0.00
Invest 10%	50,000	45,000	10,287	34,713	2,892.75	1,593	$5,000
Invest 20%	50,000	40,000	8,695	31,305	2,608.75	3,185	$10,000

Most financial planners point to pre-tax saving as the single most important thing one can do to save for retirement. Even if your funds are limited, it is beneficial. Start saving early and put away the maximum that you can. Remember—eighth wonder!

Instruments Available for Pre-tax Saving

Now that we've discovered pre-tax saving, let's examine several avenues that are available to you. There are several different "instruments" used for pre-tax savings. Their names come from various sections of the federal tax code. Think of them as baskets in which you put your money. Inside the baskets are, most commonly, different mutual funds that your employer has made available to you. Those funds can range from very conservative, like U.S. government bond funds, to more risky, like emerging market funds (read: China, Brazil, India, South Africa, etc.).

A 401(k) plan is an employer-sponsored retirement plan that permits employees to contribute part of their pay into the plan and defer taxes on that income until it is withdrawn. That is usually at retirement. There are heavy penalties if the money is withdrawn prior to age 59½. The employer sometimes matches contributions to the plan, and investment earnings accumulate tax-deferred until they are withdrawn.

A **403(b) plan** is similar to a 401(k) plan, but it is designed for public employees and employees of nonprofit organizations, like orchestras and schools. As a musician you have a greater likelihood of participating in a 403b than a 401k. These plans can also be called tax-sheltered annuities (TSAs) or tax-deferred annuities (TDAs).

A **457(b) plan** is a non-qualified tax-deferred compensation[31] plan that works very much like other retirement plans such as the 403(b) and 401(k). It is often used by highly-compensated individuals who contribute to it in addition to their 403b plan.

Tax Deductable Plans

A **Keogh plan** is a tax-deferred savings plan for individuals who are self-employed and have an unincorporated small business. If you set up a company to handle your music activities you could set aside money in a Keogh plan where money could grow, tax free, until withdrawn.

A **SEP** or **simplified employee pension** is an employer-sponsored retirement plan. Just as a Keogh plan is available to a small business owner, a SEP offers another way for funds to accumulate, tax free, until withdrawn.

IRAs come in a variety of sizes and flavors. **Traditional IRA, Educational IRA, SEP IRA (Simplified Employee Pension), Simple IRA** and **Roth IRA.** They all have their own rules, but the concept is the same. Contribute money to an IRA and it can grow, tax deferred, until withdrawn. In addition, it may also be deductible on your federal tax return. The Roth IRA is slightly different from the others in that you cannot deduct, on your federal tax return, your contributions to it. In other words, you invest funds that have already been taxed. That is the downside. The upside is that when you take qualified distributions at retirement age, they are not taxed. When considering investing in an IRA there is a plethora of information available on the web to help you choose the most appropriate one for you.

Where to Put Your Money

Individual stocks or stock mutual funds probably offer the best choice for long-term investing, since over time they have returned a little over 10 percent per year. But for the short term they are certainly not for the faint of heart. As I write this chapter the U.S. stock market is slowly coming off a nearly 45 percent decline that occurred in 2008. The optimist will say that now, everything is on sale. There are many bargains out there. For the long-term that is what history has shown. Unfortunately, our 20/20 vision only works looking into the past and not the future. So invest carefully if you're playing with long-term money, and be ready to take some lumps when the market heaves and hoes.

Where can you invest your money? Just for discussion and illustration let's take a person who is out of school five to ten years, and who has begun saving for her retirement in a

> **Lesson:**
>
> Pay down your
> credit cards first!

403b. Her long-term savings are on track for now, but she has $1,000 to invest, and plans to keep it invested for five years. What could she do with these funds? Most financial advisers say the first thing to do is to pay off the credit cards! If you owe $1,000 on a card and are paying 15 percent interest, you have to get a 15 percent return on your investment just to break even. That is very difficult to do. You need to pay down the cards—no question.

Going back to our person with $1,000 burning a hole in her purse, let's talk about some options for her.

- Keep it in her checking account

    She could certainly do this. The money would be readily available, i.e., liquid. It would be convenient. She could just go to an ATM and immediately have the cash. The downside is that on most checking accounts no interest is earned and over time with fees and inflation at 3 to 4 percent she will actually reduce the buying power of her money.

- Open a savings account at a bank

    This is slightly better than keeping the funds in a checking account, but not by much. I just called my bank and asked them the current rate that they pay on their savings accounts.

The answer was .025 percent. Yes, that's correct, a quarter of one percent. For the $1,000 that is $2.50 per year, but it is compounded quarterly so the return will be a few pennies more. The funds certainly would be safe, for the Federal Deposit Insurance Corporation (FDIC) insures them up to $250,000. This investment option might be good for a child to help her learn how to save her baby-sitting money, but not for our 30 year old musician.

- Put it in a money market account

  A money market account is the best option if she wants her funds to be readily available. Again, with interest rates as low as they are at this writing (1.67 percent at my bank), this is not a place for long-term money.

- Buy a certificate of deposit (CD)

  If our musician wants to relinquish some liquidity and tie her money up a little longer, a CD might be a good choice for her. If she goes this route she deposits her money into an account and receives a certificate of deposit that will mature and come due at a later date. She chooses the maturity date at the time of purchase and it can be from anywhere between three months to twenty years. And it's FDIC insured.

  With a CD you lock in the interest rate at the time of purchase, and generally the longer your money is tied-up, the higher the return. As I write this chapter my bank is offering a 23-month CD with an Annual Percentage Yield (APY) of 3.03 percent. There is a penalty on early withdrawal. There is also some risk, but not on losing your money, since it is FDIC insured. The risk is that CDs with longer maturities can be impacted if interest rates go up. If interest rates rise you may find yourself getting a lower return than what is being currently offered for new CDs. The longer the maturity date the greater the uncertainty. For example, if you lock in a 3 percent rate with a maturity date of five years, and interest rates go to 5 percent in three years you will not feel very good about it. The converse is also true. If interest rates go below your lock-in rate, you will be looking pretty smart. If you want safety a CD is for you, but when taxes and inflation are factored in it's pretty much a break-even situation.

- Buy Treasury bills, notes, bonds, TIPS and U.S. Savings Bonds
  These are all U.S. Treasury securities and are backed by the full faith and credit of the U.S. Government. For that reason they are generally considered risk free. They are similar to CDs in that you deposit your money for a fixed period of time and earn the rate of return at the time of purchase. They can be purchased directly from the government at treasurydirect.gov individually or as money market funds through a brokerage house.

  Here is a summary of available Treasury securities directly from treasurydirect.gov.[32]

  Treasury bills are short-term government securities with maturities ranging from a few days to 52 weeks. Bills are sold at a discount from their face value.

  Treasury notes are government securities that are issued with maturities of two, three, five, and ten years and pay interest every six months.

  Treasury bonds pay interest every six months and mature in thirty years.

  Treasury Inflation-Protected Securities (TIPS) are marketable securities whose principal is adjusted by changes in the Consumer Price Index. TIPS pay interest every six months and are issued with maturities of five, ten, and twenty years.

  I Savings Bonds are low-risk savings bonds that earn interest, while protecting you from inflation. They are sold at face value.

  EE/E Savings Bonds are secure bonds that pay interest based on current market rates for up to thirty years.

- Buy a corporate or municipal bond

  A bond represents a loan that an investor makes to a corporation or municipality. If the issuer goes bankrupt, bondholders are paid off before stockholders, so bonds are generally considered safer than stocks. Our musician with $1,000 might consider buying a bond, but I wouldn't suggest it. To make an informed decision requires a good deal of time and study. First, it may be difficult to find a suitable bond that sells for $1,000, and secondly there is no cushion if your bond's issuer has problems. With only $1,000 to invest, and if our saver is totally sold on investing in bonds, it is probably best for her to consider a bond fund.

- Invest in a mutual bond fund

  A bond mutual fund gives diversification to the investor. It invests in a large number of bonds with varying maturity dates. Diversity within the fund's portfolio lessens the risk. In addition, the fund is professionally managed. Our depositor will pay management fees, but this expertise is difficult to match by a neophyte investor.

- Stock in an individual company

  When you buy stock in a company you buy a piece of the company. As a partial owner you will gain or lose, based on the company's performance. If it does well the company may reward your ownership by giving you a dividend, and as we know, the stock price may also rise, which is good. Conversely, there is always the risk that the company may not be profitable, in which case the stock price could fall, which is bad. If things continue to decline, and the company goes out of business you could lose all of your investment, which is awful!

  A company may have millions or tens of millions of outstanding shares issued and owned by individuals, mutual funds, hedge funds, banks and brokerage houses. At various times, for whatever reason, some owners may want to sell their stock. Instead of each individual calling around to locate a buyer, stocks are traded in a central place called an exchange. In the U.S. there are three primary exchanges—the New York Stock Exchange, NASDAQ (National Association of Securities Dealers Automated Quotations) and the American Stock Exchange. The price of the stock can go up or down depending on the performance of the company. For example, if the company has a bad year the stock may go down. But other events can affect the stock. When investors or speculators look into their crystal balls and see a bright future for a particular stock or segment of the market, their enthusiasm may spread to other investors who might want to purchase that stock. This can cause the stock price to rise, since there are now more buyers relative to sellers. The opposite is also true. Bad economic news, for example, can drive stock prices down even if a specific company may be doing reasonably well.

Our investor with $1,000 in her purse should probably stay away from individual stocks. This amount of money isn't large enough to purchase a diversified portfolio. Here again, if she wants to invest in stocks, a mutual fund is probably best.

- A stock mutual fund

  There is far too much risk involved when one owns stock in a single company. In contrast, stock mutual funds offer the investor some degree of diversification by buying baskets of stocks and selling shares of the "basket." Some funds purchase stocks to replicate the entire market or a segment of the market. These are called index funds. Mutual funds come in all variations and can be conservative or risky, depending on what the "basket" contains. A fund may focus its portfolio on growth stocks, value stocks, certain types of companies (like energy, pharmaceutical or mining), stocks of a particular country or region and so on. The fund's individual philosophy and guidelines are published in its prospectus. In this document, which is distributed to investors each year, the fund officially reports how they invest the money that is put in their charge.

After going through all of the options, it should be clear to the reader that she should pay down her credit card debt, since that is the option that will yield the highest savings for her.

As I said before, investing is not for the faint of heart. Investing takes time and research, especially when one is considering stocks or bonds. You have to do your homework and make calculated decisions. Here are some hints that I have found helpful. Try to keep fees at a minimum. Look to no-load funds to help there. You can begin learning the jargon by reading the business section of your local paper, visiting mutual fund websites like Fidelity, T. Rowe Price and Vanguard or by picking up a copy of *Money* magazine. Go slowly. If you speculate, be prepared to take heavy losses. Remember, with greater return comes greater risk. However, a guaranteed way to get a 15 to 20 percent or greater return on your bottom line is to **pay off your credit cards first,** as we advised our young musician to do.

Credit Cards

Credit cards can be a convenience or a curse. They are obviously a convenience for those of us who don't want to carry around large sums of money in our pockets. They consolidate our purchases into one pay-ment, and provide a record of what we have bought. But they quickly become a curse when they are used to borrow money (read: not paid off in full each month) because they usually carry very high interest rates.

> **Lesson:**
>
> Don't use credit cards to borrow money. Pay them off in full each month if you can.

"According to Nellie Mae,[33] the average undergraduate has $2,200 in credit card debt. That figure jumps to $5,800 for graduate students. Since so many student credit cards have high annual percentage rates, often at higher rates than the rest of the population, given their thinner credit files, the longer these students wait to pay the cards off, the more money they'll pay in the form of interest."[34]

It's no secret that credit cards are aggressively marketed to students, and in some cases the schools facilitate this by entering into exclusive marketing agreements with the companies. With easy access to these cards, and a *laissez-faire* attitude about their use, it is easy for a student to accumulate a small mountain of debt even before he or she graduates and has a job. Here are some alarming statistics from Erica Williams' testimony in June 2008 before the House Financial Services Subcommittee on Financial Institutions and Consumer Credit for college-age young people at 18 to 24 years of age.[35]

> * According to a 2004 study by Nellie Mae, 76 percent of undergrads have credit cards, and the average undergraduate has $2,200 in credit card debt. Additionally, they will amass, on average, almost $20,000 in student debt.

> * Another study found that 18 to 24 year-olds in 1989 devoted 13 percent of their income to debt payments. Today's 18 to 24 year-olds devote 22 percent of their income to servicing their debt.

> * One-fourth of the students surveyed in US PIRG's 2008 Campus Credit Card Trap report said that they have paid a late fee, and 15 percent have paid an "over the limit" fee. Credit card companies will often impose a "penalty rate" of 30 percent or more after just one or two late payments, and this interest rate will often last for six months or more. Sometimes, customers are charged a penalty rate because they were late on a different loan (this is called "risk-based re-pricing" or "universal default"), and some banks manipulate the due dates from one month to another to rack up late fees.

What is even more alarming, and frankly difficult to believe, a 2006 poll of three million young people in their twenties, conducted by *USA Today* and Experian, the credit-reporting agency, found that "nearly half of twentysomethings have stopped paying a debt, forcing lenders to 'charge off' the debt and sell it to a collection agency, or had cars repossessed or sought bankruptcy protection."[36]

It's easy to blame credit card companies for our financial woes, but at the end of the day it is the individual who must take responsibility. Just recognize that these companies are aggressive, and their goal is to make it easy for us to accumulate debt. Accept it, and adopt the following strategies to use credit cards more effectively—and to your benefit.

- Use them to defer payment for a short time.
- Don't use them as a loan. The rate is too high.
- Watch out for annual fees, finance charges, late fees and grace periods.
- Shop around for the best interest rates. Use the web for that.
- Don't fall behind in your payments.
- Always pay something on your balance, and do it on time.
- Once you get the balance down, try to pay it off each month.
- Keep a good credit rating.

Insurance

Everyone needs it, but we usually hope that we will never have to use it. Insurance protects us and our families against relatively minor events, like a cracked automobile windshield, or major events like the unexpected death of a family's primary breadwinner. Some insurance is mandatory. If you have a house with a mortgage, the bank requires it to be insured against fire, theft, and other casualties. This makes sense because banks want their investments protected. The same is true for auto insurance. At least in New York State you must show proof of insurance in order to register your vehicle and get license plates. For insurance that is non-compulsory, like health and life insurance you should first determine if you need it, calculate how much you need and do research to find an insurer that is right for you.

Instrument Insurance

Musicians need instrument insurance. We can't afford to be without the tools of our trade. If you go through the company that insures your home or your car, be prepared to pay very high rates, and that's assuming that they will agree to insure you in the first place. A better way to insure your instrument(s) is with companies that specialize in this. Clarion Associates, Inc., Total Dollar Insurance and Heritage Insurance are three such firms. Shop and compare prices. For expensive string instruments make sure to look at Total Dollar. If you are a member of the Musician's Union, Clarion will give you a discount, but you should check the other companies as well.

Health Insurance

Most people get their health insurance as a benefit through their job, but for freelancers and young people just graduated from college there can be a limbo period. My daughter's boyfriend, who eventually became her husband, found himself in that situation when he graduated from college. He was looking for work in his field, but until he found his first "real job" he worked as a grounds keeper in a city park, a job he had had during summers. There were no benefits, so he had no health insurance through the park job. He could have been added to

Lesson:

Explore all available options for health insurance before going without.

his parent's policy but the cost was very high, and getting a policy of his own was no better. Being in what he thought was good health, he decided to go without insurance, hoping that he would soon find a job with health benefits. This turned out to be like playing Russian roulette, which didn't work for him.

He began having digestive tract problems, but the doctor originally diagnosed it as nerves. When his condition worsened he found himself in the hospital, which turned into a ten-day stay, and when he was released he was presented with a $12,000 bill. Since he had no insurance, the hospital counseled him and he was directed to a New York State program for help, but he didn't qualify. He owed the $12,000.

This is a stark lesson: if you don't have health insurance and you get sick, the hospital and your doctors do not forgive whatever debt you incur. It is an obligation that must be met. "Declare bankruptcy," one might say. That decision should be your last choice, because it will affect your credit standing forever. Even though Chapter 7 Bankruptcy is expunged from your credit report after ten years, and Chapter 13 after seven, the reality is that it stays with you for life, since many loan and job applications ask if you have ever filed for bankruptcy. With bankruptcy off of the table, my now son-in-law began a payment program to pay off the debt. He says it was like a loan.

Unfortunately, his digestive tract problems turned out to be Crohn's disease, and now with a good job and benefits that provide health insurance, he is covered. That's a good thing, because the treatment he now takes for this disease costs $8,000 per session—every six weeks!

If you find yourself in this limbo world of the uninsured, there are a couple of options you can explore. Group insurance is cheaper than individual insurance. If you teach at a school, but do not qualify for their health benefits because you are part time, you may be allowed to join their group and pay the full premium. The Musician's Union has a group plan and it has turned out to be a good solution for many needing health insurance. A third alternative is to check into COBRA (Consolidated Omnibus Budget Reconciliation Act). It was put into place by the U.S. Congress in 1986 and gives certain employees the right to continue group health coverage that otherwise would be terminated. You have to pay for it and it is generally more expensive than previous insurance, since you have no employer paying part of the cost. But it is worth looking into to see if you qualify and if it is competitive with other alternatives.

Life Insurance

If you are 25 years old, on your own and single you probably don't need life insurance, but if you are 25, married, have a child and you are the primary breadwinner, you do. You don't purchase life insurance for you. You buy it for those who survive you in the event of your death. A stay-at-home parent should also have at least a small policy to cover childcare.

The most cost effective way to purchase life insurance is to buy term insurance. That is pure insurance—a certain dollar amount for a set time period—for example, $300,000 for 30 years. Insurance salesmen will often steer you toward policies that have a cash value, since they make a higher commission on them. These policies have names like whole life, ordinary life or universal life. They have an advantage over term insurance in that as long as the premiums are paid, the protection is guaranteed for your life. This can be a good thing, if for some reason you develop a condition that affects your insurability. These policies also accumulate a cash value that over time can grow. The disadvantage is that whole life is more costly than term insurance. Importantly, the return is also generally lower than what can be realized from other investments. These cash value life insurance policies represent what many would consider an antiquated way of thinking. They were bought by your grandparents in the days when the insurance man would come to your home to collect the monthly payment. Today's more enlightened thinking recommends that those who need life insurance would be better off purchasing term insurance and saving for retirement through other means.

CHAPTER 9

Five Non-Linear Career Journeys

THIS CHAPTER SPOTLIGHTS four individuals and one ensemble that have attained success in their respective corners of the music world. They are all currently at the top of their game, and yet their career journeys are far from over. I've devoted a chapter to them because in terms of achievement in music they have far surpassed the norm. They aren't superstars or "famous" people to the general public, but within their field they are well known and respected. To me they are simply everyday people I'm happy to call friends. They each faced many of the same issues and challenges that young musicians face today, but these talented, creative persons illustrate the foundational lessons of this book: set your goals and figure out how to get there. As each of these artists traveled from their own point A to point B, they contributed their unique legacies to the industry. We begin with Maria Schneider.

Maria Schneider–It's Not Your Father's Record Business Anymore

Maria Schneider is arguably the hottest jazz composer going right now. Her debut recording *Evanescence* was nominated for two 1995 Grammy Awards. Her second and third recordings, *Coming About* and *Allégresse,* were also nominated for Grammys. In addition, *Allégresse* was chosen by both *Time* and *Billboard* as one of their Top Ten Recordings of 2000, inclusive of all genres of music. *Concert in the Garden* was released only through her website (an ArtistShare® site) and won a 2005 Grammy for "Best Large Ensemble Album." It also won "Jazz Album of the Year" by both the Jazz Journalists Awards and the *DownBeat* Critics Poll, and Maria was named "Composer of the Year" and "Arranger of the Year." But in spite of all these awards, it is even more impressive that *Concert in the Garden* was the first recording to win a Grammy with Internet-only sales! What was Maria's evolution as a composer and bandleader that has led to these accolades, and where does she go from here?

Maria was born and raised in Windom, a small farm community in southwest Minnesota, a town with a population of 3,600 where the clothing store also sold records. When she was five, a woman, who Maria would come to know as Mrs. Butler, moved to Windom from Chicago. She was a musician who played classical as well as stride piano. When Maria's parents heard about her, they invited her to come over for dinner after which she played the piano. In Maria's words, "The music just rose out and became this separate entity. For me, life went into living color at that moment." Maria began studying with Mrs. Butler and found her to be an amazing teacher. She would talk to her about how music was made, and what makes it sound the way it does. This led to Maria's interest in composing. Soon it was time to go to college, and thinking that being a composer was too lofty a goal and that her piano playing was good by Windom's standards, but not up to the rest of the world's, she decided to be a theory major.

The University of Minnesota was a good fit for her. She studied orchestration with Dominick Argento, but it was Paul Fetler who noticed her interest in jazz and urged her to check out the jazz ensemble. Maria began observing their rehearsals, but since there were no jazz courses other than the jazz ensemble, she basically taught herself with some tutoring by one of the band members and by reading Rayburn Wright's, *Inside the Score,* a popular jazz composition and arranging book of the time. Wright was the Eastman School Jazz Department Chair and a widely respected arranger/composer/teacher. Maria set her sights on attending Eastman for graduate school. She applied but was turned down. Wright recognized Maria's talent, however, and told her that all she lacked was experience. He suggested that she attend the Arranger's Workshop that was held at Eastman in the summers, which she did. In the meantime Maria was accepted into the program at the University of Miami, but going to Eastman and studying with Ray had been a dream of hers. She applied to Eastman a second time, was accepted and earned a master's degree in jazz composition.

Decision time. School was over. Now what? She wanted to try New York. She had copyist skills so she figured the copying would pay the bills and she could still compose. At that same time she applied for and received a grant to study with Bob Brookmeyer and soon after became an assistant to Gil Evans. She was working with her musical heroes. Being around them made her realize that one reason they were successful was because they had devoted their lives to developing their own voice, their style and their sound. She decided it was time for her to start her own band.

And so, in 1993 and every Monday night for five years, Maria's jazz orchestra could be heard at Visiones, a club in New York's Greenwich Village. Her musicians made $25 a night and she made $15, plus she had the honor of schlepping the music and stands, getting the band together, finding subs, setting up, breaking it down . . . It was a labor of love. She didn't realize it at the time but she was not only developing her music, she was actually doing something called "fan building"—creating a following for her, the band and her music. All the while she continued to work as a copyist. In fact, during the first eight years in New York she made her living entirely from copying and not from composing.

Brookmeyer introduced her to a radio orchestra in Europe and from that, other European gigs began to come in. Before she knew it she was busy in Europe and she didn't have to copy anymore. She was making a living as a composer. Visiones eventually closed, but by that time her reputation had grown to the point that she and her band were doing short concert tours.

She decided to make a recording, so she began looking for a label, but there was not much interest. They all said she wasn't marketable.

Undeterred, she decided to do it herself. She gambled with $30,000 she had saved, and made a recording. She shopped it around and again nobody wanted it, except for a small company in Germany. They agreed to pay $10,000 for it. She felt lucky that at least it was going to be out there for sale, and to make it even better this company was known for the high quality of their products. She felt fortunate to have found an interested party. Maria made three records for the German label. She was happy with the quality of the recordings, but disappointed in the financial payback. She had put blood, sweat and tears into each recording, but the way artist royalties are calculated and subtracted from recording costs and advances—called recoupment—she wasn't making financial headway. She felt there had to be another way.

Maria was in Germany when she got a call from her friend Brian Camelio, "Maria, what's something that nobody can file share?" Maria said, "I don't know Brian, what?" He said, "The creative process. I'll use the Internet. I'm going to create something where we document the creative process of making a recording. And you'll announce ahead of time that you're going to make this record, and we are going to video it, and you're going to talk about what you do. We're going to come back and find out who all your fans are, and I'm going to build this thing."

Maria thought he was crazy. She was still thinking that the Internet wasn't that big a deal. When she returned home they talked about it. They started going over the numbers, and their conversation went something like this:

"Look," said Brian, "by going directly to your fans we don't need a record company. I'll be the record company and I'll take 15 percent. But we're not going to pay the distributor; we're not going to pay the record store. So what could you sell a CD for?"

Maria replied, "I don't know $16, $17?"

"Okay, so we'll pay the credit card fee and I'll get 15 percent. Look at your profit margin. What if we had donors? We could have gold, silver, bronze participants and they get all this extra stuff, and they get to be named on the CD. What if we have an executive producer and he can come to the recording session? What if we have things for composers?"

It took a couple of years to build, with a lot of talking and planning, but Brian created ArtistShare® and Maria was his first artist on the site. Within the first couple of weeks after its launch they had their first gold participant signed up—for $1,000. People started pre-ordering. That first record, *Concert in the Garden,* cost $100,000, and was quickly paid for. Amazingly, it went on to become the first Grammy winning record to be sold only on the Internet.

Early on, Brian recognized an important point and instilled it in Maria. His company, ArtistShare,® creates fans and not just customers. By becoming privy to Maria's creative process, her fans buy into and become a part of the project. If you sell your product in a record store it is an anonymous sale. But if you sell through your site, you have the buyer's email address. By collecting and building her email list Maria has her fan base at her fingertips, and when she wants to do a project she can immediately contact them.

Not only is the ArtistShare® model good for the musician's business, she believes it is also good for the music.

> I think that the ArtistShare® model is really good for the music, because it makes you feel how important your customers, your fans, are. You have to treat them with respect and the thing that Brian has been pushing with me, which I think is really true, is that today no one just wants to buy music. They can get it for free. And what's more revealing is that everybody believes they're entitled to get it for free. What's important is creating a relationship with people. That's what they want—a relationship with the artist. The days of being an artist and just staying in your corner practicing and not relating to people are over. Look at a musician like Yo-Yo Ma. He's such a music ambassador. That kind of thing is natural for him. It's something you really can't fake.[37]

Maria's career continues to evolve and build on itself. She isn't content with the status quo, and she continues to stretch herself and take on new challenges. In the fall 2008 she took a step into the "classical music" world when she premiered a work for Dawn Upshaw and the St. Paul Chamber Orchestra. It will be performed in Carnegie Hall in 2011. She has a project in the works with the Kronos Quartet and has aspirations to do a theatre and possibly film work if the fit is good. She recognizes that as she moves into different areas, she'll have to work at keeping her band going. But just as a good parent never abandons an older child when a new one comes along, I suspect that Maria will always have her jazz orchestra. It will always be her baby.

What are the lessons from Maria Schneider's story?

1. Don't give up on yourself. 2. Invest in yourself. 3. Keep your eye on the prize. 4. Work toward a goal. 5. Don't be afraid to take calculated risks. 6. Don't be afraid to do something that hasn't been done before. 7. Keep your art at a high level. Don't dilute it. 8. Look for and recognize opportunities. 9. Today, consumers can get music for free. They want more than just the music. 10. Don't be embarrassed about making money. 11. Be the best at what you do.

Todd and Chandra Lowery–We Want to Live Here. How Can We Make a Living?

Todd and Chandra Lowery were newly married, both having graduated from the Eastman School in the early '90s. Chandra is a pianist, and Todd plays trombone and composes—mainly jazz. Chandra, who has an American father but whose mother is Japanese, had a strong desire to experience the Japanese culture firsthand. And so, being young with no solid roots put down, they decided to move to Japan. It would be temporary—maybe staying just a year. Chandra got a job teaching English in the Japan Exchange and Teaching Programme (JET) and, given a choice of locations, decided to accept a position in Gunma prefecture (read: state). It was only 90 kilometers north of Tokyo, and through the advice of a musician friend who was freelancing there, Todd felt it was close enough for him to commute and that he could find work there. So they began their adventure in Japan.

The first year went well for both of them. Chandra was teaching English and Todd started picking up work and meeting people in Tokyo. They also began playing small gigs together in schools around Gunma. A beautiful concert hall had just been built, and since it was new, it was underutilized and could be rented for a very reasonable amount. So they decided to put on a concert. They produced it themselves and mainly through word of mouth they sold 1,000 tickets! The concert featured both of them in various settings—solo piano pieces, duos and a jazz quartet featuring musicians Todd had worked with in Tokyo. The success of the concert led the management of the hall to hire Todd to produce a second concert and bring a name jazz artist to Japan—pianist Kenny Werner.

Time marched on and soon Chandra was in the third and final year of her contract. A decision point was looming ahead. What to do? It seemed like they had three options: move back to New York, move to Tokyo or stay in Gunma in the town of Kiryu, where they lived. But just at this time, a major earthquake devastated Kobe. The Kiryu town fathers asked Todd to put on a benefit concert to help in the relief, and they chose an old sake warehouse as the venue. The town fathers also had a secondary motive; they wanted to show the residents of Kiryu that this space could be a good performance venue. As you might suspect, the concert was a success and the warehouse, called Yurinkan, was renovated into a beautiful art space.

Following that performance Todd and Chandra quickly became part of the Kiryu community. They were often in the newspapers and had many supporters. At the urging of friends they decided to stay in Kiryu and try to create an arts scene. It seemed like the most interesting choice. Todd was busy playing in Tokyo, but as he became more involved in the musical life of Kiryu the phone started to ring less. More and more he turned the Tokyo work down, but he found that it didn't bother him too much. In Tokyo he was a sideman; in Kiryu he was working on his own projects.

In his words, "Events are like fireworks. Lots of activity and fanfare, then it's over." He wanted to do more than just one-off performances, so he started a jazz series with a concert every other month. Each concert had a theme, and since it was 1997, he began a countdown to the twenty-first century by working his way through jazz history. He brought in soloists from the U.S. and Europe. The concerts were educational as well and always included commentary. The series still goes on today. But the Yurinkan is a much smaller space than the hall in which he held his first concert. It's more intimate with 80 to 120 people the norm. Although the series is fun and rewarding, he couldn't make a living solely from it.

Chandra's JET program was coming to a close, so after careful thought, they decided to set up their own English school. Chandra had no problem with a visa since her mother was Japanese, but Todd had some difficulty. With $30,000 borrowed from the bank they set up a company, a limited corporation, and with Todd as president and CEO, his visa problems were circumvented and he was allowed to both play and teach. Their school, *Harmony*, was created and one subject was taught—English.

Harmony was private and not part of the Japanese system. The students attended in the evenings and on weekends, and both Todd and Chandra taught there. Todd even arranged tours and took his students to the U.S. on field trips. There was a market here. In Japanese schools the students must take English, but it isn't taught conversationally. Students might be able to read it, but they can't speak it. It is difficult for us to imagine, but Japanese businessmen who want to practice speaking English would often take Todd and Chandra out to dinner, pay for the meal and pay them additionally for their conversation.

Todd borrowed $20,000 from the bank and made a CD, which increased his exposure. He also quickly paid off both the loan for the school and the CD. His credit was very good. The school grew—50 then 100 students. He hired another teacher. Now what? Of course—start a music school! That was always his long-range goal. After all it was what both he and Chandra had gone to Eastman to learn how to do.

Todd contacted the architect who had renovated the Yurinkan and together they visited the oldest textile factory in Kiryu. It was abandoned and run down, but both men saw its potential. It was famous because the first Japanese exported silk came from there. This would be a perfect building for what Todd and Chandra had in mind. It took a year to obtain permits and to negotiate with the family that owned the building, but the bank eagerly lent the money for renovation, and Todd had his school.

Just before the opening of the music school, Todd told all his English students that, if they wanted to take an instrument, he would teach them at no charge for two months. Of those who took him up on it, 90 percent continued lessons. Today both schools combined have more than 200 students. Since the students primarily take their lessons after school, the music school also functions as a concert space and during the day as an art gallery. Not only does the art that is shown beautify the space, it is also for sale with a commission of 20 to 40 percent going back to the school! (And it's high-end!) The "artsy" atmosphere is a plus for the music students' parents, since it provides a pleasant ambiance in which to wait for their children.

Musically, Todd was interested in using Richard Grunow's and Christopher Azzara's instrumental method, *Jump Right In.* He felt that good music education was lacking in Japan. He observed that many Japanese people believe that music is something you experience and not necessarily learn or study. He also found that many have the attitude that the purpose of education is to get a job and not to improve your life. He began volunteering at area schools and he was welcomed, but many teachers would simply take a break and not watch what he was doing. Part of the problem was with them. In Japanese elementary schools the teachers teach all subjects, including art, music and physical education. Because they are expected to be generalists, most Japanese teachers don't teach music with much depth. They play records and sing songs; the students learn the names of the notes, the treble and bass clef, but not much beyond that. Todd and Chandra found another gap to fill in Japanese music education: when students take instruments they don't practice. In Japan, taking music lessons is like taking ballet or swimming. You practice when you are at your lesson but not at home. It was a frustrating mindset and very different than what they expected.

Then one day Todd heard that the mayor of Ota, a nearby town, was starting an English immersion school. The then Prime Minister of Japan, Mr. Koizumi, had instituted a deregulation policy to stimulate the floundering Japanese economy. It encouraged entrepreneurial activities. Though it wasn't meant for education, the Ota mayor, Mr. Shimizu, applied for and received permission to create a Free Education Zone and with it this new school. In itself this was revolutionary because in Japan the curriculum is the same throughout the country. From north to south the same textbooks and materials are used, and the same tests are administered at the same time of year. This new English immersion school would allow for different texts and teaching techniques to be used. Todd was immediately on the case and contacted the mayor whom he already knew from his concerts. Long story short, Todd was hired as part of the planning committee and helped design the curriculum for the entire school.

The school began with grades one to four and added a higher grade every year. Currently there are seven grades. Every student plays an instrument and begins its study in the fifth grade. There are 108 students in each class and unlike in the U.S., the drop out rate is quite low. Chandra was also hired to teach general music, and a third teacher rounds out the rest of the music department. Eventually there will be grades one to twelve, and there is even talk of a college. The unique thing about the school is that the students receive a Japanese diploma even though they do not study the national curriculum. This is the only public school in the country to be allowed to do that.

The second distinctive feature from a music perspective is that the *Jump Right In* method is used. This method features rote learning, but not just parroting back what the teacher plays. Students use their ears to develop their musicianship, and they don't learn to read music right away. They also learn to improvise. Think of the way an infant learns language—imitation, learning words, putting them together, then reading. It's the same progression with this method—imitating what the instructor plays, conversing through improvisation, then reading music.

I believe that much of Todd and Chandra's success can be attributed to their willingness and ability to be assimilated into the Japanese culture. They could not have achieved their success without it. Still just in their early 40s, they have many years ahead of them to see where this journey will eventually lead.

What are the lessons to learn from Todd's and Chandra's story?

1. You don't have to live in a large metropolitan area to have a fulfilling life in music. 2. It is possible to choose a place to live and then create your musical life around it. 3. Become part of, and contribute to, the community. 4. Make friends and acquaintances. 5. Look for and recognize opportunities. 6. Be the best at what you do.

Jeff Tyzik–What's in My Lego Kit?

Jeff Tyzik began his musical career in Hyde Park, New York, at the age of nine when he started playing the cornet. By the seventh grade, he knew that he wanted to make music a career, but he had no idea what that meant. He hadn't really talked to anyone about it or sought out a counselor. All he knew was that music was the most important thing in his life. The bands of Woody Herman, Buddy Rich, Maynard Ferguson and Count Basie were still criss-crossing the country giving concerts, so by the time Jeff was in high school he had heard the road bands that came to town. Popular radio stations of the day played music that, if not 100 percent jazz, had a jazz flavor to it. There were trumpet players on the radio and television and he wanted to be like them. They were his role models. So, upon the advice of a friend, he applied to the Eastman School and was accepted.

While a student at Eastman, Jeff played in bands that gave him a taste of what club life was like. As he grew older his desire to be a jazz musician started somewhat to wane. He found he was also interested in composing, conducting and teaching. His musical horizon was broadening and so were his employment opportunities! But relatively early on he realized something that was very perceptive and profound. He understood that his idols at the time, Miles Davis and Freddie Hubbard, were unique individuals who became jazz icons not just by being great players. It is true that their paths to recognition and eminence were totally distinctive and based partly on their musical skills; but their success was also due to factors not readily apparent to those of us who simply stood in awe of their success. We knew nothing about their contacts in the music business, for example. In essence, their success was partly a great mystery. But by this point Jeff had some familiarity with the inner workings of the music industry, and he saw that even if he reached the performance level of a Miles Davis or Freddie Hubbard, there would be no guarantee that he would be as successful as them. In fact, most of us who have been around a while can recall numerous "great" players who never "made it" in the business. As only a player, Jeff knew his opportunities would be very limited, and so he decided to use the many Legos in his kit and widen the scope of possibilities for his career. For him, just being a jazz trumpet player ceased to be a viable option. Nevertheless, he did go through his solo trumpet phase and had four albums that were picked up by Capital and Polydor.

Jeff was a recording artist with a major label, but he soon discovered that, due to the way the accounting is structured, it was going to be nearly impossible for him to ever make any money doing it.

(I have to take a break from Jeff's story at this point to discuss **advances and recoupment**. If a record company gives a $10,000 advance, for example, it is not free money. They want to get that back and they do it by a process called recoupment. The advance puts the artist in the red—a deficit. The artist must pay the record company back until the advance is paid off. At the point when the account is in the black the artist will then begin receiving royalty checks. In reality he or she has been receiving royalties all along, but they have not gone into his or her pocket. They have been going into the account to pay off the deficit.

Now here is the important part of this explanation. If a CD retails for $20, the record company may make $5 per CD. Out of that the artist may make $1 per CD in royalties. At $4 profit per CD one might think that when the company sells 2,500 copies the advance would be paid off [$4 x 2500]. But that is not the case. *The recoupment is against the artist's royalties.* In other words, if the artist gets $1 per CD, 10,000 CDs must be sold to pay off the advance.

Recording costs are also recoupable and that can include a long list of things like equipment rental, arrangements and even catering and limos. These costs can add to the deficit in an account making it even more difficult to ever get back to even. It's like racking up charges with a credit card and only paying off the interest. Now back to Jeff.)

So, he realized that the odds of ever making his livelihood strictly as a jazz artist were against him, but he had other talents (read: Legos) on which he began to draw. He composed music for radio and television commercials, short films and TV themes (Lego). He was developing his studio chops. He was composing and hearing back almost immediately what worked and what didn't (Lego). Early on at Eastman, Jeff was introduced to Doc Severinsen through Allen Vizzutti. A friendship developed that led him to do orchestra arrangements for Doc's concert appearances (Lego). It was there that he realized he could do that too. And in addition, because of his knowledge of the trumpet, he felt he could do it better. Through his relationship with Doc, he was also discovering what worked and what didn't in live performance (Lego). He was learning. A second professional opportunity developed. Chuck Mangione had been the jazz ensemble director at the Eastman School and Jeff was one of the standouts in the group. When Chuck began doing dates with orchestras, Jeff was asked to play in the trumpet section (Lego). Because he was eager and talented, he soon found himself joining Mangione in the studio, which eventually led to co-producing four Mangione albums (Lego).

Through his close associations with Severinsen and Mangione, Jeff saw an opportunity. He felt he could combine his conducting, trumpet, arranging, composing and producing skills with his good business sense to develop something that was somewhat unique within the Pops orchestra field. He didn't know it at the time, but he was developing a business model.

He had a product: Jeff the conductor, performer, composer and arranger. He had ideas about using the product: concerts. He needed research on these ideas: what are orchestras playing? What works? He had to develop the ideas: create concerts and programs. Lastly, he had to sell his ideas (read: concerts). His process was very business like. Product—how to use—research—develop—create—market.

An initial venture into the orchestral world as a featured performer and composer was with trumpeter Allen Vizzutti. Together they created *High Class Brass,* a concert that combined classical, jazz and Latin music in one package. Audiences and musicians alike enthusiastically received it. This concert turned out to be a virtual test marketing of Jeff and Allen's musical philosophy and, more importantly, laid the groundwork for Jeff's conducting career that was to follow.

Soon, Jeff had several concerts under his belt with smaller orchestras, and in the meantime he was always thinking of what could come next. His first big moment of opportunity came when he sat down with the Artistic Administrator of the Rochester Philharmonic Orchestra (RPO) and presented himself and his vision. He had carefully thought through and created four programs, and knowing that budget is always an issue, he crafted the concerts with that in mind. He kept his fee low. He created and played up the concept of orchestra as a family, by using the musicians as soloists. In his presentation he projected a total picture of what he was capable of doing, and in the process he gave the RPO a vision. It worked and he was given his first shot at a concert with the orchestra. Predictably it was a success, and Jeff was offered the position of Principal Pops Conductor of the RPO for the following season.

Jeff had observed, from attending Pops concerts of several different orchestras, that in general the musicians did not look happy. In many cases they were playing corny music that was sometimes almost a caricature of orchestral repertoire, often without musical integrity whatsoever. (After all, what piece doesn't sound better with a duck-call or slide-whistle in it?) So—from day one it became his mission to develop an audience that had as much passion about the Pops series as the classical audience had for the classical series. He targeted the delivery as the issue. Not that you couldn't have fun, but first and foremost he wanted music and artists that would lift the human spirit. He also recognized that there are many people who want to experience a symphony orchestra but for various reasons (intimidation by the space, formality, etiquette, other people, etc.) are reluctant to attend a classical concert. Jeff decided to make it part of his mission to help educate orchestra administrations who seemed to think that "Pops is an easy way to make music, and the dumb people come to Pops concerts. Let's give them this watered-down version of what we really want to do, and maybe if we're lucky we can get them to come to classical concerts."

Jeff's mission was to put on concerts with musical integrity and to create an audience that thinks of the Pops series as fondly, and takes it as seriously, as the classical audience treats its series. This philosophy and premise created his niche in the orchestral world. But it isn't always easy. Many times he is working with administrators and consultants who think of Pops concerts as Las Vegas style headline acts with the orchestra as wallpaper. Their creativity is usually limited to how many different Broadway concerts they can concoct! They are also frequently averse to building a new series. A particular concert or type of music may get one shot and if it doesn't do well it's back to the tried and true.

There can also be initial pushback from musicians as well. But they come around if they are given the chance to play music with integrity—whether it's classical, jazz, country, blues, big band, Latin, you name the style. If there is something in the music for them to latch on to and commit to, they give it their all. But not if the music is wallpaper or badly written—they just check out.

When Jeff came to the RPO he didn't just do what was expected. He went beyond his job description. He took it upon himself, and it was not part of his contract, to be a part of every series: Pops, Education (including Elementary School, Middle School and High School programs) Community Outreach Concerts, The Orkidstra series (family concerts) and eventually the main-stage Classical Series. His reasoning was that if he was going to represent the orchestra as a spokesman, as he was often asked to do, he needed to fully understand the different orchestra worlds in which he had to function, and how the organization could and did serve the community. In order to be an effective leader, he needed to know, first hand, how each series worked and how it related to the overall mission of the institution. Over the years, these varied experiences with the RPO cemented his overall vision of how to make the symphony orchestra more relevant in today's world.

Jeff first used his trumpet Legos to create a career. It ran its course. But he recognized that in the meantime he had been developing a new set of Legos that led him to the Pops orchestra field. One might think that the years he spent on the trumpet/recording artist path were lost years, but quite the contrary. He had been developing a national reputation as someone who did quality work. The typical Pops concertgoer didn't know him yet, but he had developed a base awareness within certain musical circles and was a known entity. His success as an arranger/composer and producer lent credibility to his desire to be a conductor. When he turned his direction 100 percent to conducting he wasn't starting over. He was simply correcting his career course. Using a nautical metaphor, instead of steering his boat due north he steered it northeast—same boat, same compass, different direction.

Today Jeff still uses talents and skills honed years ago as a trumpet artist and producer. He brings into play his arranging and composing skills by writing the music for many of his concerts. This creates tailor-made events. He avoids the Pops concert model of the orchestra as Las Vegas backup musicians by featuring soloists within the orchestra. This creates goodwill among the musicians, and he produces recordings for many of the orchestras with which he has a relationship. No other Pops conductor of which I am aware can do, or is doing, these things.

When one thinks of Jeff's brand today it encompasses many things. When you hire him you get *a solid conductor* with musical veracity, *a creative artist* who comes with his own great arrangements and compositions, *a warm personality* who can connect with an audience, *a bold leader* who is willing to take a calculated risk and *an accomplished professional* who always delivers a quality product.

Now at the top of his game and still rising, Jeff looks to composing and conducting the classical repertoire for personal reward and growth. He continues to receive commissions for orchestral works, and in Rochester he has been given opportunities to conduct on the Philharmonic Series. One thing is certain. He will continue to evolve and grow. That's what makes his life interesting and keeps him energized.

What are the lessons to learn from Jeff Tyzik's story?

1. Don't give up on yourself. 2. Keep your options open. 3. Your best career fit may not be the first one you attempt. 4. Evaluate your Legos. 5. Be realistic about career possibilities. 6. Don't be afraid to take calculated risks. 7. Keep your art at a high level. 8. Look for and recognize opportunities. 9. Build your audience and don't pander to them. 10. Don't just deliver what is expected. Go beyond your job description. 11. Be the best at what you do.

Robert DiLutis–Invest in Yourself

When Robert was in fifth grade his father, who was a trumpet player, came home with a clarinet for him. It didn't work, but instead of saying that he wanted another instrument, Robert said, "How do we fix this?" They looked at the instrument and the pads seemed bad. They looked "funny" and were "hanging off." So, his father got some pads, brought them home, and Robert took the clarinet apart. He replaced the pads, not knowing anything about how to properly do it. He used Elmer's glue! After it was back together the moment of truth came, and low and behold . . . it didn't work! (Did you think he was going to hit a home run the first time up to bat?) Undeterred, Robert was off to the library to look for books on instrument repair. He found a well-known one by Erick Brand and, carefully following its instructions, got the clarinet in working order.

That was the beginning of his repair business, and by the time he was in middle school he had a little shop in his basement where he worked on his classmates' instruments. This seemed natural to him since not only was his father very handy around the house, he also had one uncle who built grandfather clocks and another who repaired watches. Tinkering and mechanical skill were in his blood.

Robert didn't just repair his instrument. He practiced it. All along he took lessons, and when he was in seventh grade the Peabody Institute came to his school and auditioned interested students for scholarships. Both Robert and his brother, John, received scholarships and they began their study in the pre-college division. He continued to be interested in the way things work, which made middle school with its shop classes very compelling to him. In high school he was fortunate to have a great band director with a fantastic music program. The Perry Hall High School in Baltimore, Maryland, was a school of 1,200 students, of which 600 were in the music program! The marching band was 350 strong. There were three concert bands, two orchestras and three choruses. The band was actually run by the students. The band director, Clinton Marshall, knew how to delegate authority, and students had certain jobs assigned to them. In his freshman year Robert was put in charge of uniforms, and by his senior year he was the band president.

Robert's interest in mechanical things and fixing things were hobbies. His main focus was practicing and he was obsessed with it. His teacher, William Blayney, encouraged him to go to Juilliard and study with David Weber, which he did. As a freshman at Juilliard, he formed a trio and as starving students they started looking for gigs. Their first gig was playing in a restaurant for dinner. They kept playing and playing—at first, always at these entry-level gigs. Gradually, they moved up the food chain, started doing competitions and won the Artists International competition. Building on this success, they made a successful Carnegie Hall debut recital. The trio repertoire is limited so they arranged, transcribed and adapted music from other sources. Ten years later, after each had gone his separate way they put the music into a book and published it!

After graduation from Juilliard, Robert took a job teaching at the Baltimore School for the Arts, practiced, played some shows and took auditions. Two years and seventeen auditions later he won his first orchestra job—this one with the San Antonio Symphony. Since he was new to San Antonio and had no students, he had more free time. He started making his own reeds. He had tried using reed-making machines before, but they weren't satisfactory for him. He wanted something better so he began to think and experiment. He had the idea of somehow hinging a reed knife onto a moveable apparatus that would copy an existing reed in a manner similar to a key-making machine. He drew up some plans and took it to a machine shop. Luckily the folks there were patient with him. They knew he didn't know anything about precision machining, but together they worked on a prototype. After nearly a year, and several versions that weren't quite right, they finally came up with something that worked. That summer he went to the International Clarinet Convention armed with a pamphlet showing a picture of the machine and a price—$400. He had no vendor booth. He simply walked around and passed the pamphlets out. Almost to his surprise people began to order them.

He decided that he needed to protect his invention. Through a casual conversation with another parent at a Pop Warner Football League game, he met a man who had invented a coffee cup lid that didn't allow the contents to spill when the cup is knocked over. He helped Robert through the patent process. The Reed Machine, as he called it, was his first product, but he also had other ideas. He had created other tools to help finish the reed—profilers and planers. With patents costing $5,000 to $10,000 the problem with the smaller, less complicated tools was that he couldn't make them inexpensively enough, or sell enough of them, to make money. And some things are just not patentable. Reed cases, clarinet pegs, drum sticks and the like are all generic. A Patent Pending Application (PPA) protects his most recent invention, a reed clipper. For $50 this latest patent option will protect an invention for one year while the inventor does more research to determine its economic viability.

Robert was in the San Antonio Symphony for five years and in his second year he, his wife and two other orchestra members decided to start a music school. They had all attended pre-college divisions of good music schools and recognized the value of this experience for high school students. There are a few small colleges in San Antonio, but they had no pre-college music departments for young students. They saw an opportunity. They talked to area band directors and interested teachers, and gave it a summer test run with clarinet and jazz workshops. They attracted more than 100 clarinetists and 75 jazz students. The interest was there, so it was full steam ahead. They talked the college into letting them teach in one of the buildings that wasn't used on weekends. Using their affiliation with the symphony they were able to draw on its musicians for student referrals and teachers. The first year they had 50 to 70 students, whom they taught on Saturdays and Sundays. But San Antonio is not a wealthy city and many of the students needed scholarships. They needed an angel. Through a father of one of Robert's students, who was a Certified Public Account, they were able to use his offices from which to run the business. He would also occasionally help out financially when funds came up short for a student or two.

The school took off and in the second year they had nearly 200 students signed up. They went to pawn shops and bought pianos, keyboards, music stands, everything they could find that they needed. The school quickly grew. Interested jazz musicians who wanted to start a jazz department approached them. This made sense, and the jazz program was started. They formed a board and filed for 501(c)(3), not-for-profit status. The faculty was up to twenty plus. But Robert was still interested in moving to a more stable orchestra. When a job in the Rochester Philharmonic became open, he auditioned for it and got it. Robert, his wife and stepson left San Antonio, and with that the leadership of the school was gone. Their absence, along with the symphony's financial problems, which forced many of its musicians to find work in other cities, contributed to the eventual demise of the school.

In Rochester, Robert continued to play in the orchestra. He expanded his business by adding a line of clarinet barrels. Even a relatively small, uncomplicated product like a clarinet barrel requires a lot of oversight and up-front money. The tolerances have to be exact. There is laser engraving. The wood has to be purchased and shipped from Africa. To ensure quality control and to be able to get the product when he needs it, he has them made in Rochester, Wisconsin and Prague. Robert's business problem is that whatever money he brings in has to be used to pay for more product that is being manufactured. He must invest in himself, and that can be a little scary in the current economy. He may have 30 people who owe him money, and in turn he owes money to his suppliers, and they owe money to their suppliers. When the chain gets broken, it affects everyone else in the chain. In Robert's case he has to be careful about over ordering. He doesn't want to get stuck with an over supply of product that isn't selling. However, his products are sold globally and when one market is down there are usually others that are not doing as badly.

Robert calls playing the clarinet in the orchestra his home base. Companies would refer to this as his core business. And he is smart to know that he has to keep his core strong. Because of this, he allows himself only four hours per week to work on his projects. It's the combination of playing, experimenting and inventing that gives him the greatest satisfaction. He says that if he only performed he wouldn't be as happy as he currently is doing a combination of things. His desire to learn how things work motivates him to experiment. He obviously receives money for what he does, but that isn't what drives him. It's curiosity. It took six prototypes and a lot of money to get his reed clipper working the way he envisioned. Most people would give up, but tenacity is certainly one of Robert's greatest assets. Always looking forward, Robert recently accepted a clarinet professorship at Louisiana State University and has begun this new stage in his life.

What are the lessons from Robert DiLutis' story?

1. It is possible to be good at more than one thing. 2. Be curious. 3. An idea is just an idea until you act on it. 4. Don't be afraid to take calculated

risks. 5. Don't be afraid to do something that hasn't been done before. 6. If you believe in something see it through to the end. 7. Look for and recognize opportunities. 8. Take advantage of personal connections to make business connections. 9. Create "projects" in areas that interest you. 10. Keep your core business, in his case playing the clarinet, at a high level. 11. Invest in yourself. 12. Be the best at what you do.

Alarm Will Sound—More of a Band Than an Orchestra

Alarm Will Sound (AWS) was established in 2001, and its first concert was in May of that year at the Miller Theatre in New York City. But there is a pre-history to be told. Around 1996 and while they were still students at the Eastman School of Music, Alan Pierson, Gavin Chuck and four other Eastman students created Ossia.[38] It wasn't really a new music ensemble, but rather more of a production company. They saw a need and wanted to present concerts that would feature large ensemble works of student composers as well as some minimalist composers whose music they felt was underperformed at the school. For them it was also an opportunity to learn concert production through practical experience. At that same time, the Eastman faculty and administration was rethinking its curriculum, and a series of courses designed to bridge the gap between the "ivory tower" and the real world were taking shape—the Arts Leadership Program. Ossia's idea of artistic excellence and real-world experience was a perfect fit for the Eastman culture of the time, and they found immediate support from the school's administration.

The experience of forming Ossia and putting on concerts helped several of its members to discover other heretofore unknown talents. Gavin Chuck, for example, whose doctoral study was in composition and theory, found that he liked and had a knack for organization and artistic administration. Alan Pierson came to Eastman as a composition major but through Ossia became passionate about conducting and switched to that major for his doctoral work.

Ossia was very much a group effort. Built into its mission was the thought that they would solicit ideas for programs and repertoire. They wanted to keep their ears close to the ground and program what their audience (read: their peers) actually wanted to hear. But the college years go by quickly, and soon Ossia's members found themselves about to step into the real world. They decided to take the momentum that they had created with Ossia and carry it forward. They created Alarm Will Sound.

Where Ossia was a quasi-production company, Alarm Will Sound is an ensemble. It works differently but still makes use of many of the fundamental lessons learned from the school group. Gavin Chuck credits much of the success AWS has achieved to the fact that the AWS musicians more or less grew up musically together. They were all students at the same time. They had common interests. They were friends. Together they were learning about both the managerial side and the performance side of music. Basically there have been very few personnel changes since its beginning in 2001. These personal relationships have been the glue of the group, and the members of AWS think of themselves as more of a band than an orchestra.

To them a band is more about personal commitment to one another, and these bonds allow them to push each other artistically. Consequently, they do more interesting things than what a typical pickup ensemble might do. In the real world, large ensembles that play new music are essentially made up of freelancers whose commitment to each other is basically just for that gig. They may play very well, but what AWS brings to the table is a more adventurous concert experience, which is a direct result of the friendship and trust within the group.

Collaboration surrounds the planning of each concert, when the players bring repertoire and program ideas forward for discussion. When the idea was proposed to arrange some of the music of Aphex Twin for the group, it was met with mixed support. About half the room was not convinced that this was a good idea, but because they were friends they heard each other out and eventually went with the idea. This music resulted in their concert and CD, *Acoustica,* which was a hit and successful on many levels. This kind of risk taking is definitely found more with bands than orchestras.

Consensus building and discussion also contributes to group owner-ship. Anyone who has been a leader of just about anything has experienced the feeling of responsibility for the success or failure the project. With AWS the members are free to contribute and discuss artistic as well as administrative decisions, and each individual feels a responsibility for the group. There is buy-in. Each time they get together for a performance or series of performances they have a group meeting where organizational and artistic issues are discussed. They confer and brainstorm. It's not a democracy as such, since with the exception of bringing in new members to the group and selecting the winner of their composition contest, they don't usually take votes. But with the group's input, Alan and Gavin are trusted and empowered to make most final decisions. To permit a balance of flexibility with commitment to the group, substitutes are allowed; but there is a policy that no member can miss more than one third of the productions in a single year. In addition, one-year leaves of absence are also allowed without forfeiture of position in the group.

When they formed in 2001 they were excited knowing that they would fill a niche. There was no new music group of their size (18 players) touring nationally that had the reputation of Ensemble Intercontemporain, for example. On the other hand, they knew that one of the reasons that an opportunity existed was because of the expense involved. So they agreed at the outset to pay themselves a nominal fee of $50 each per concert and to contribute the rest to startup costs. Only as owners could they do this. The fee was low, but at least it was something. As with most performing musicians their income stems from many different sources so no one in the group is reliant on AWS concerts for their sole support. Their real payment comes from the joy they get from playing music they love, and are committed to, with friends. Fortunately, as their reputation has grown so has their fee.

Once they realized that their musical and organizational concept worked, they briefly considered making AWS a full-time gig for every-one, but the idea didn't go very far. The musicians had already begun to establish their own paths, and it was obvious that a big change in personnel would probably have to take place. There was also the economic reality. With a group this size there is a limited number of venues and markets that can support it. Their decision was to do eight to ten productions a year, basically getting together once a month. This work schedule has proven to be positive rather than negative. The players look forward to getting together, they remain fresh and interested in the music, and the time between gigs allows for creative headspace to imagine and develop new productions. Because they are a large group, there is always the pressure from venues—wanting the AWS name but not the AWS cost—to attempt to negotiate for a concert with fewer musicians. But early on AWS decided that from a brand perspective they would not break up into smaller units. AWS means a large group of musicians—the same musicians each time, playing new music, and often in unique and unexpected ways.

The administrative staff is extremely lean. It is structured with an artistic director, Alan Pierson, and a managing director, Gavin Chuck. There is a production manager, Jason Varvaro who is in charge of logistics, and he makes sure all the musicians and equipment show up when and where they are supposed to. From the outset the group wanted to perform in a way that clearly engaged the music and the audience. As a result they have a staging director, Nigel Maister. Not all of the pieces they play are staged, but when they feel that an extra performance element is called for, they call on Nigel. A small stipend is set aside for development work with donors and friends of the organization. In-kind gifts are appreciated and often received from individuals or organizations that want to donate rehearsal space or equipment.

The name Alarm Will Sound has an interesting story. As Eastman students, Alan and Gavin would work out together at a local gym. One day they were both on exercise machines, which were directly in front of the emergency exit door. You guessed it. The sign on the door was *Alarm Will Sound*. A light bulb went off in Gavin's head. He liked it because the phrase captured some of the things they were talking about with their new group—a sense of adventure, something unpredictable or even dangerous. It was somewhat unusual so journalists might be able to do clever things with it, and it had the word sound in it; but one disadvantage was that it didn't tell anything about the makeup of the group. Gavin became the advocate for it. It was put in the mix of possible names, and in perhaps the only time the group ever voted on anything, Alarm Will Sound barely squeaked by and was chosen as the ensemble's name.

The group has no publicist or booking management. Their philosophy is that if they put together interesting concerts and present them at the highest possible musical level, the concerts/productions, themselves, will generate a buzz and attention. The programming and repertoire do the work of a publicist. So far it has worked. Their concerts have a coherent idea behind them. *Acoustica* features music originally written for electronic instruments arranged for acoustic instruments. The central theme of "a/rhythmia" is music with rhythmic complexity and includes an orchestration of a player-piano piece that is impossible to be performed by human hands. They created a multi-media event with *1969,* which tells the story of composers and performers in the year 1969 responding to the spirit of the times. Interesting concerts like these grab the attention of the press, because they are not simply one nice piece followed by another nice piece, followed by another nice . . . This is how AWS describes *1969* on their website.

> February 1969, the German composer Karlheinz Stockhausen planned to meet The Beatles in New York City. Their aim was to develop a joint concert, one which would have transformed the cultural landscape, uniting the popular and concert music worlds as never before. But a blizzard shut down the city, and while Stockhausen reached the meeting point, The Beatles never arrived.

> Alarm Will Sound's *1969* is a unique multimedia event that tells the story of great musicians—Stockhausen, Lennon, McCartney, Berio, Bernstein and Stravinsky—striving for a new world and a new music in the tumultuous months surrounding the assassinations of Martin Luther King Jr. and Robert Kennedy and the election of Richard Nixon.

> With the contagious we-can-remake-the-world optimism
> of 1969 now a distant memory, Alarm Will Sound's *1969*
> offers a relevant evening of entertainment.[39]

Once a program is developed it becomes part of their repertoire and is performed at multiple venues. This cuts down on rehearsal time for programs in their "standard repertoire" and also allows them to work on new programs. In the beginning AWS established themselves in New York City, often playing at the Miller Theatre. Their goal has always been to tour nationally and internationally, and each year their reach has increased to include other U.S. cities and international festivals.

As they look into the future they want to continue to envision themselves as performers in the fullest sense and to challenge themselves with more complex productions. To date, *1969* is their most multifarious production. Its staging, acting, use of video, choreography in the loosest sense of the word, singing and of course playing in a scripted, concert-length story make it unquestionably complex, but they fully expect that when looked at in their rear-view mirror 10 or 20 years from now, it will seem just one step along their evolutionary road.

From an organization standpoint they want to increase their fund-raising capacity. Ticket sales pay for about 75 percent of their operating expense, which is good for a group of their size, but a larger donor base would allow them to be paid better. It would also allow for the hiring of a full-time administrative staff.

Their advice to young groups wanting to remain together in the professional world is to use ideas that make sense with the music to create compelling concerts. Don't just slap together programs of pieces you like. Go beyond that to engage both yourselves and your audience, and use your education to stimulate imaginative thinking. The second thing is to recognize that music is a performing art. Just the notes are not enough. Properly executing the pitches and the rhythms do not equal a performance. They are important but cannot be the end. And third, in terms of forming and maintaining ensembles, it's not arts management, but people management. Creative people come in different shapes and sizes, and their leaders must be socially aware. AWS doesn't view the musicians as interchangeable. When you get AWS you don't just get a clarinetist, cellist or percussionist, etc. You get Bill, Stefan and Payton. Their success has largely been built on its members and the bond and chemistry that has been established. Alarm Will Sound is unquestionably more of a band than an orchestra.

These five stories represent five different paths to "success" in music, but they share some commonalities. Out of curiosity, I looked at the "lessons" that I assigned to each story, and sure enough there were some recurring themes. For me these "lessons" represent the entrepreneurial spirit, and in my mind are good life lessons for all of us.

What are the lessons from Alarm Will Sound's story?

1. In musical groups the whole can be greater than the sum of its parts. 2. You may not know it now, but many of the people you meet in school will be working with you for the rest of your career. Keep the networks going. 3. Make your performances events. 4. The notes aren't enough. 5. Don't be afraid to do something that hasn't been done before. 6. All members of a group should be stakeholders. 7. Protect your brand. Don't dilute it. 8. Go cheap at the outset. 9. Have goals. 10. Think big. 11. Be the best at what you do.

Recurring Lessons From These Stories

- Be the best at what you do.
- Look for and recognize opportunities.
- Don't be afraid to do something that hasn't been done before.
- Keep your art at a high level. Don't dilute it.
- Don't be afraid to take calculated risks.
- Don't give up on yourself.
- Work toward a goal.

CHAPTER 10

Ninety-Six Street Level Tips That You Won't Learn in Most Music Schools

WHEN A MUSICIAN MOVES FROM the student world to the professional world, the rules change. In real life your superiors, friends and business associates will not wake up in the morning and ask themselves how they can help you and your career. School's out! If you have worked hard and have talent you are most likely a good player. But being a good player is only part of the package that you must put together to be successful. Equally important in making the transition into the "real world" and eventually getting ahead in music most likely has as much to do about your personal and social skills as your musical ability.

What They Don't Teach You at Harvard Business School, by Mark H. McCormack[40] was a best-selling book from the 1980s. It was written by an entrepreneur who founded a company and in the process, in his words, "ended up giving birth to an industry—the sports management and sports marketing industry." As I read his book, 25 years ago, I recognized that many of the topics that he talked about were directly applicable to music and still remain relevant today. So I adapted this format for musicians and began including it in my *Entrepreneurship in Music* class at Eastman. In the previous chapters of this book you may have noticed that I have highlighted particularly important "lessons" for you—things I didn't want you to miss. In this chapter I'll just give it to you straight. This chapter is nothing but lessons. What follows are some, mostly non-musical, street-level tips and things to think about as you launch your career as a professional musician.

Being a Professional

Do Your Own Thing, Then Figure Out How To Get Paid For It

I once was invited to be part of a panel discussion at the International Trombone Association's annual convention. The subject was orchestra opportunities for trombonists. When I arrived at the venue, I looked at the sessions and concerts that had gone on in previous days, and I saw that a sackbut quartet had given a concert the night before. (The sackbut is a precursor to the modern trombone and dates from the fourteenth century.) I thought to myself, "What is that all about? Those guys must get together once a year and haul out their sackbuts and jam. They can't make any money at it!" I voiced this thought to the trombonist friend of mine who invited me to the conference, and to my surprise at the time (but not now in retrospect) I learned that those guys are in demand all over the world! They were on their way to Europe right after the conference. They are doing their own thing. Their music is too specific to do it full-time in Des Moines or Denver or even New York City, but they apparently dominate the sackbut world market, and they do very well playing the music they love, on these old instruments, for lots of people.

Think about Béla Fleck or Jake Shimabukuro—banjo and ukulele virtuosi, respectively. They have taken their particular instruments and put them into musical contexts that were previously unimagined. The lesson for me is to do your thing, *very well*, and then figure out how to get to the audience that wants to hear you and is willing to pay for it. It's not that big a stretch if you are very, very good.

Make Friends–Your Peers Are Your Best Resource

Think about it. It's only human nature to recommend a friend for a job. Putting aside the fact that if you recommend him or her, he or she may reciprocate one day, it just feels good to help out a friend, provided they are a good fit for the job. Even though music is a highly competitive business, it's best to put rivalries aside. You and your buddies may be going for the same type of work, but the pie is usually big enough to accommodate the good players. I have often joked that I've made a career of collecting the crumbs off the table after everyone has left. I've had some good composition and arranging commissions based on recommendations of others who were either too busy or not that interested in accepting the work. "One man's trash is another man's treasure." Who said that?

Be Yourself

As a professor and former department chair at the Eastman School I've been a part of numerous faculty searches. I can remember one, in particular, when we were looking to find a successor for a retiring performance faculty member who was a giant in the field. We narrowed the group down to three or four and invited them in for a couple of days of interviews and teaching. The candidate who I am thinking of was a personable, younger man (for this job) in his forties. He was an "up and comer." The afternoon came and the candidate played a short recital, which was very good. Next came the master class. As he coached the students his personality appeared to change. Suddenly he took on a persona of a wise man, a jedi master, an Obi-Wan Kanobe type. Maybe he was trying to be as profound as the person who was retiring, but it didn't fit. He seemed to assume a role that he thought was "how you do it at Eastman." The result was not successful at all. He was clearly not being himself. Needless to say, the committee was not impressed.

Know the Players–Size Up the Situation

Among any group, regardless of its size or its purpose, there are some who stand out from the pack. They are the influencers—the leaders—the players. When I attended Michigan State I had a scholarship to play in the band, but to keep it in the fall semester I had to play in the marching band. That required me to arrive on campus a week or so before the start of school. Coming from Colorado I didn't know a soul, but during the lunch breaks, which we all took together, I noticed a table that was really having fun. I could tell. They were the "cats"! It didn't happen that first week, but relatively soon thereafter I introduced myself to one of the guys, and before long I was "hanging" with them. My first impressions turned out to be correct. They were the influencers.

Why is it important to "know the players"? I would argue that if one is striving to be the best, it's important to know who is on top and leading. In any city, find out who are the most respected musicians on your instrument and why. If you are a new member to an orchestra or a school faculty, size up the situation and determine who are the positive people, and stay away from the negative, disgruntled ones.

Try Not To Be Noticed

Remember earlier when I said it was important to *be noticed?* Well, here is an instance when you don't want that at all. When you get that first call to play in any group that is already established—i.e., a symphony orchestra, pit orchestra, jazz group, church choir, etc.—your job is to fit into what is already going on. Each group has its own culture, and orchestra musicians in particular often find little ways to "goof around" in rehearsals, especially if they are very familiar with the music, or if they don't have a lot of notes to play on a particular piece. The jokes are subtle, and only those close by even know that this banter is going on, but don't be tempted to join in. Just take care of business. *You aren't in the club yet!* It's not stated anywhere, but you are on probation. Your brand (remember when we talked about that) should be all about competence, reliability, flexibility and professionalism. From a musical standpoint, if you are subbing and playing an inner part, your job is to fit in and provide support to the first player.

In a related instance, just recently I was in an orchestra rehearsal. The trumpets weren't goofing off, but they were fiddling with their phones—text messaging, surfing the Internet, playing games. Who knows? The conductor stopped the orchestra and said, "Trumpets, send yourself a text message to come in at letter C!" Busted!

Don't Lay Low–Be Noticed

In an earlier chapter in this book I described how, when I arrived at Eastman as a student, I decided to audition for the large ensembles. I wasn't required to play in them because I was a Doctor of Musical Arts (DMA) student and playing the large ensembles wasn't part of my course of study. But since I was new, I realized that the best and quickest way to meet people was to play in these groups. I wanted to get my name out there and start working around town.

As a new kid on the block you must make connections. Call old friends and acquaintances in the area and renew your connections with them. Find out who are the influential musicians in town. What kind of work do they do? Who's doing now what you would like to be doing in the future? Try to connect with them. Maybe they'll need a sub at some point. You can always "take a lesson" from them, but when individuals contact me to do this I am usually turned off unless they are serious about learning what I have to offer. If they just want to play for me to show me what they can do (read: impress/audition for me) I'd rather have them say that upfront.

You can always ask your teachers for names of their former students in the area to which you want to move. Get the names of contractors. Call or write them and introduce yourself. If they are interested they may ask for a recording and résumé. You never know about this. Sometimes contractors get stuck and the right call at the right time just might result in some work for you. (Hint: Make sure you can deliver the goods and are ready to handle whatever style or type of music you are pitching. If you get an opportunity and don't live up to what you purport to do, it could be a long time before you ever get a second chance from that person. Remember about your brand and how it can be tarnished.)

If you graduated from college, contact your alumni office and ask them for names of alums in your area who play your instrument. We help our graduates with this at Eastman. I imagine that other schools do the same.

Don't Play Lead from the Second Chair

This is important to remember. The second and third players defer to the principal on most things. Even if your tuner says you are sharp, accommodate your pitch to that of the section. Blend in with the group. Cool out on the vibrato. Balance and listen. Don't show them how well you can play your part by projecting over the others. It's very distracting (and unmusical) to have a player on an inner voice who is over-playing. And when warming up don't ever play the principal player's solos. That's a definite capital offense, and you'll be punished for it in some way down the road.

Don't Look at the Soloist

Maybe you have experienced this. You are in an orchestra or other large group and someone behind you has a solo. You must resist the impulse to turn and look to see who is playing, particularly if it isn't going very well. Solos, even the small "easy" ones, can become very difficult if the player starts losing confidence. Little distractions can undermine the performance. If the person next to you has a solo, don't fidget, turn pages, or swab out your instrument. No distractions.

Look at the Soloist

Now, in jazz settings the rules change. When a player has a solo the focus should be on him or her. My first gig with the Buddy Rich band drove this point home. At least once in every set Buddy would have an extended drum solo. It didn't take long for me to notice that the entire band's eyes were glued to him. I don't know if he told them to do it, or if it happened naturally, but I certainly got the message without it being openly stated. Turn around. Look at Buddy.

Show your friends some respect when it is their turn to shine. It is very distracting (read: rude) to see two musicians talking on stage when someone in the group is soloing. (P.S.: This usually happens during the bass solo!)

Control Your Nerves

I usually find it more nerve-racking to play a two-measure solo in an orchestra concert than to play a full recital. In a recital if something doesn't go exactly the way you want, it's your problem, but you still have the rest of the recital to redeem yourself. In an orchestra, on the other hand, you are part of a group, a team, and if you screw up there is a feeling that you let the other players down.

Here is what used to happen to me in my early days of orchestra playing. I would take my seat and play over my solos or exposed passages. Play it once—perfect. Try it again. Perfect—no problem. I would play it a third time and a fourth time, trying to see how consistent I was. Eventually I would mess it up. Can't leave it that way—try again. Messed it up once more! Now the concertmaster has come on stage and there is no opportunity to play it once more. The last time I played the passage I screwed it up! That is not a good way to go into a concert. What I do now is this. If the solo is lyrical I play a few problem intervals in it that I want to make sure are well connected and legato. I might make up a little exercise around them. I don't play the solo in its entirety, but I think it through. If the passage is technical I play it through slowly, reminding myself of the notes. I move my fingers like little soldiers. I might play it once, but I resist the temptation to play it many times. I want to make sure that the last time I play that solo it is good and secure. That works for me.

Of course the best way to control nerves is to be absolutely prepared. That's the best way to build confidence. But when something does happen and a misstep occurs, you have to immediately forget about it and move on. It's not that you accept sloppy playing. What you accept is that you can't be perfect all of the time. We aren't machines. With that said the really top players are amazingly consistent and predictably steady. That is what we strive for.

Learn To Deal with Stress

Musicians have the usual everyday stress of work and life, as well as the anxiety of performance. Let's talk about everyday stress first. We all have stressful moments during each day. Something sets us off and we can feel our temperature and blood pressure rising. Some of us have chronic stress, which can lead to all sorts of health issues. There are many proven stress management techniques out there that I encourage you to look into, but I'm no expert in the area. With that said, in my everyday life, I do try to do a couple of things to reduce my stress. I try to only worry about the things that I can influence. I try not to dwell on things over which I have no control. I also try not to get bent out of shape over small inconsequential events. You can only fight so many battles, so you must choose the ones about which you are truly passionate. Here are some things we should probably do to reduce stress, but often don't: exercise, meditate, do deep breathing exercises, have realistic expectations of ourselves, have a positive outlook on life, accept change, know that perfection is really never attained and good enough does not have to mean mediocre.

Then there is stress related directly to performance and playing an instrument. Orchestra musicians, particularly those in principal positions, probably feel this more than any other subset of musicians, for, as said before, most will tell you that a little four-measure solo in an orchestra produces more anxiety than playing a full solo recital. There is tremendous pressure (probably self-inflicted and exaggerated) to play "perfectly," to not "spoil the entire piece" and to not let the others in the group down. Some players get into serious "head games" and lose confidence to the point where their performance is seriously compromised. A string player's bow may chatter as he plays a sustained note. A wind player may look for a special new fingering to solve a specific problem only to combine the new fingering with the old one with disastrous results. Brass players can lose consistency to the point where even the "easiest" solo has the potential for a cracked note. The answer for some is drugs.

You have probably heard of beta-blockers. Propranolol is the generic drug in this category, and it is sold in the United States under the brand name Inderal. You, or someone in your family, may take it to lower high blood pressure. Who knows how musicians became aware of this drug. It was probably by accident, but it is well known in the music world. It doesn't pump you up, increase muscle mass or give you any supernatural performance powers. It doesn't improve anything. If you can't play the part before the concert begins, you will not be able to play it after you take one of these pills! It simply cools you out and strips away debilitating symptoms associated with stage fright. It will help stop your embouchure (read: mouth/lip position on the reed or mouthpiece of a musical instrument) from trembling, or your hands or fingers from shaking. They simply lessen anxiety and symptoms associated with performing (read: nerves).

You can imagine that the use of these drugs is controversial among musicians. Some are adamantly opposed to their use, while others view them on the same level as taking an aspirin to relieve a headache. But, as with most drugs, there can be side effects. If you do experience debilitating stage fright, and it continues over a period of time, you should consider discussing this with your doctor. You need to be fully informed and aware of the pros and the cons. But don't take any drugs given to you by a friend or associate especially if it is directly before a performance. You won't know how your body will react to the drug.

Personally, I like to be pumped up a little and on my toes for a concert. I've found that the best treatment for nerves is to be absolutely prepared and confident. That is easy to say, and even seasoned players can experience anxiety, but the more a musician performs the more self-assured he or she will become.

Be Nice to the Stagehands

Stagehands make an orchestra musician's life easier. They are at the concert hall well before us and they remain long after our portion of the event is over. They make it possible for us to walk in, sit down and do what we do—play music. They are a resourceful lot who pride themselves on taking care of our requests, often in creative ways. (I once forgot a black bowtie. A stagehand made one for me out of gaffers tape!) But, sometimes our requests can seem somewhat petty. "Can I have a higher chair?" "My stand-light bulb is flickering." "This monitor is too loud." I've found that stagehands will go out of their way to help those who have taken the time to establish a relationship with them and avoid those who take them for granted or emit a superiority-vibe. They are part of the team and deserve respect for their contribution to it. Give it to them.

Give Compliments, Take Compliments

Musicians like to do a good job. It feels good to play your best, but it feels even better when others recognize it and compliment you. Often, particularly if we feel we haven't played up to our best, we can give a cold shoulder to an admiring audience member. Take the compliment even if you think you ruined the concert. What they heard, they liked. If you go into a play-by-play recounting your botched performance, it can make your admirer feel like they don't have enough musical sophistication to know good from bad.

On the other hand, giving compliments should be natural and unforced. Every player seems to need support. If your colleague sounded great in a particular performance, let him or her know you heard and appreciated it.

Give Credit

Giving credit to those responsible for the success of a project is oftentimes the most important thing a leader can do. Musicians often work in the not-for-profit world where salaries can be, on the whole, less than corporations. Employees work in the offices of an orchestra or music school often because they like the arts or just being around artists. Their payment for a job well done is not always measured in financial remuneration. It's in recognition. For them there is nothing worse than a person who has had little input into a project but "shows up at the finish line for pictures." Giving credit to all those who help make an event a success is very important. It will make them want to work hard for you, and it reaffirms their importance as a contributor to the organization. Even the maintenance man likes to work for a winner.

If You're a Jerk You Had Better Be the Leader

If you are this type of person (and I realize that most people who fall into the jerk category don't even think of themselves in this way), you will find it very difficult to get work. You may get hired once, but repeat calls may be slow in coming. It's human nature. We want to be around those with whom we get along, and since 99 percent of a musician's work-life is spent playing in groups of two or more, it is essential that we learn to leave the egos at home and work cooperatively together. This is just common sense. If I have a choice between hiring player A or B, and both are equal in skill, I'll hire the one who is accommodating and flexible. Those who do the hiring have enough to worry about without the added hassle of dealing with a high-maintenance person. We'll hire them, but only when we're stuck. Hmm . . . let's see . . . difficult person, doesn't get many calls . . . You can always be a leader! You will get to hire anyone you want . . . but then you'll have to deal with clients. On second thought, better develop some people skills.

The Union Is Your Friend

I recently received an email signed by a dozen or so Eastman students. It was sent to Eastman School jazz students and faculty. This group had met out of frustration. It seems that within the student jazz community at Eastman, there has not been much discussion or communication between them about how to contract gigs, or for that matter how much to charge. This had resulted in a wide range of prices charged for the same type of work, and as a result there has been a considerable amount of unintentional undercutting going on. Some bands were not rehired to play at certain clubs because another group would play for less. The musicians who met and drafted the email proposed several minimum wage scales. It occurred to me that they were, in effect, forming a union.

This is what unions do. They establish minimum pay rates and working conditions. They help organize and protect the musicians. They have standardized contracts, and if an employer tries to renege on paying, the union will stand behind the musicians. The other major function of a union is to gain legal representation on behalf of a group of workers (read: employees) and then negotiate directly with the employer on their behalf. Examples of this are orchestra contracts, contracts with specific performance venues and various recording agreements such as: sound recordings, industrial films, theatrical motion picture, television film, basic cable television, commercial announcements and National Public Radio.

Unions help take the "Wild West," every-man-for-himself mind-set out of the mix. One often hears the comment, "What has the union done for me? They haven't given me any work." That could be true, but the union's job is not to hand out work. It is to protect its members from what I just described.

I think unions are good. I have a nice little pension due to the recording work I have done, and I have good working conditions in the orchestra in which I play. For a professional musician, unless you are a soloist, most of the "good work" is union work.

Avoid One-Offs, Get Mileage Out of What You Do

As we age we begin to realize that time is precious. Time to practice, to be with family, to work on a career. In graduate school there were certain assignments or projects that I had to do for school. I didn't want to put in a lot of time on something only to have it go into storage upon completion. So I started to think of ways the work I was doing for class could also be published either in its entirety or edited in a manner that would make it suitable for publication. With this kind of thinking I was able to extract four articles from my doctoral dissertation, another one from a lecture recital and even a wind ensemble piece from an orchestration class. I've tried to have the attitude that if it's worth doing, it's worth sharing with others. In other words, publishing.

If you work your tail off getting a difficult piece ready for a recital, try to find another place to perform it. Book some studio time and record it. If you are in school and don't leave at graduation with a good recording that is representative of what you do, you've wasted an opportunity. Do good work and look for ways to get the most mileage out of it.

Don't Worry about the Other Guy

My friend Maria Schneider has described this very well. "If you are a student, and especially if you are at one of the top schools, you are one of many persons who are just as talented as you. It's the same in the professional world. There will always be someone who can play faster, higher and louder than you. It can be inspiring, but it can also kill something in you. You can begin to compare yourself to your peers. 'Why am I a musician? I'm not good enough. I have nothing to say. So and so is better. I'm never going to make a living. What am I thinking? Who am I? I'm nobody.' You start thinking these things and before you know it you've completely lost any kind of attachment to that first thing that made you want to be a musician in the very beginning. It's very important to reconnect to that because that's the thing that's alive and abundant." Remember what made you want to become a musician. We all can remember that moment. Keep that spirit going and don't worry about the other guy.

Be a Life-Long Student

It is important to realize that school does not end when you graduate. It may be corny and cliché, but successful people continue to be curious—to check out new things—and to adapt. They remain life-long students. Your business (You, Inc.) has to be built on your playing (singing, composing, teaching or scholarship) and should revolve around your strengths and interests. If you keep growing as a musician you will never get bored or complacent.

Write Down What You Know

When I was a student I had a notebook that I took to my lessons. I'm sure I didn't think of this myself. One of my teachers probably told me to do it, so I did. Over time I collected nuggets of wisdom from several teachers. When I first started teaching privately, I simply regurgitated what my teachers had taught me. It was good information and it worked. There was nothing wrong with that. But one day I started thinking, "Why don't my students just take lessons from my teacher and get all this good information first hand?" That's when I started thinking about the way I do things when I play. Of course I took what former teachers had taught me and used it—sometimes verbatim. After all each generation builds its knowledge on the shoulders of the preceding one. But soon I began to develop my own ideas and techniques and to incorporate them into my own teaching.

One of the courses that I taught early on in my career was jazz improvisation. At that time improvisation courses for college credit were not that common, and, in addition, there were only a handful of published books on the subject. This was a blessing in disguise for me, since it forced me, in consultation with my colleagues, to develop my own curriculum. I wrote down what I knew and what I was discovering in the classes that I taught. Whatever I was developing in my classes was also being validated or rejected there—sort of test-driven by my students. Going under the assumption that whatever was good enough for my class was good enough to share with others through publication, I ended up publishing several books that each year still continue to sell very well.

Writing down what you know makes you think critically about what you do. You can revisit those thoughts years later. This is especially important if you are a teacher or have private students. Remember, an idea is just an idea until it is written down.

Have an Idea/Project File

If you are like me you get ideas all the time—melodies for tunes, bass lines, pieces that would sound good transcribed for various instruments or ensembles and ideas for compositions, you name it. My problem is remembering later in the day that great melody I was humming when I got up in the morning. So, I have an idea file. I write things down, keep them in one place and when I have some free time and I'm looking for a project, I consult the file. It works for me.

One Thing Leads to Another

In music it is quite true that the various professional projects we undertake are all intertwined. For example, most jazz players also compose. Composing helps the improvising, and improvising helps the composing. Everything you do professionally can contribute to and help when the next opportunity arises. As you put your career together you will find this to be true. For example, you are more likely to be successful in obtaining a grant if you have published an article, released a CD or written a book. These things all beget each other. Grants beget grants, books beget other books and articles, articles beget other articles . . . and so on. If you are interested in higher-education teaching all these things beget your first job, a better job or a tenured job. If you are curious and have a mindset that anything worth figuring out is worth sharing with others, these things will come naturally and without forcing them. The important thing is to adopt this mindset.

We Know You Will Be a Teacher

As musicians, nearly all of us will teach on some level. From those of us who teach public school, college or private studio, to others who are primarily performers like Renée Fleming and Yo-Yo Ma who may only do occasional master classes, all of us teach. In learning our craft there is a certain amount of "in the trenches, by the numbers" work that is necessary just to develop the skill to control our instruments. But there is also the creative side that has to be nurtured and allowed to blossom. I would argue that an "open head, pour in knowledge, take the test" style of teaching is necessary to some extent in order to develop chops (read: technical facility), but *allowing artistry to blossom is really the key element.* No matter what instrument students play or the style of music they are interested in, encourage them to play by ear, play what they hear, compose, create, take apart, analyze, have an opinion and develop their own voice. This will help them separate from the pack and escape the "musician as commodity" classification. Our students should not all sound the same. Their personalities should shine through. Robots are good for assembling cars, but not for music.

Don't Talk Money in Front of Others

This seems obvious and just common sense, but you'd be surprised how often it happens. Money matters are best discussed in one-on-one conversations and not in groups. The fact is that often not everyone will make the same money on the same gig. Certain players ask for and deserve premium pay, while others may have doubles[41] that raises their salary. Public money discussions can make everyone feel uncomfortable. In our culture we generally don't talk openly about how much we make. Save these discussions for private talks, and don't put the leader or contractor in an awkward position.

Don't Talk About Upcoming Gigs in Front of Others

Picture this scenario. You're on a freelance gig and standing around on a break. One of the guys says, "Are there more particulars on that gig next month for United Services?" Immediately all those who haven't heard about the gig or been hired for it will start to wonder, "What gig? Why haven't I heard about it? Is so-and-so mad at me? What else have I not been hired for?" and so on. This puts the leader or contractor on the spot, which can get uncomfortable. Maybe they will be hired but the contractor just hasn't gotten to it yet, or maybe the required instrumentation doesn't include the same or the usual musicians. I've noticed that people often ask tactless questions like this just to let others know that they are busy and working. Not everyone needs or wants to know how busy you are.

Know the Difference Between Honesty and Tact

There's an old joke by either Rodney Dangerfield or Henny Youngman. I can't remember which. It goes something like this. A doctor is just finishing up a physical examination. He says to the patient, "I'm sorry, I have bad news for you. You have two weeks to live." The man replies, "That's impossible. I want a second opinion!" The doctor comes back, "Okay. You're ugly too!" It's a corny joke, but it illustrates a point. The doctor is honest, but he has no tact. We all have had interactions with persons who for some reason lay their opinions right out there. A nice way of saying it is that they are "direct." Often after dropping a bomb they follow it by, "I was just being honest." As musicians we ask our friends and associates all the time their opinions on our playing. It can go something like this. "Was I okay on that solo? I felt sharp. How was it?" Or, "I was lost for a line or two in the second movement. Was it obvious?" You should be honest, but with a little tact. As a teacher I choose my words very carefully. Unless the student really needs to be knocked down a peg or two, I try to give the good with the bad, and to end with a positive spin. When a colleague asks for your opinion give it honestly, but don't tear him or her down.

Make Sure You Can Back Up What You Say

When you get a call from someone who has never hired you before, they are hiring you based on your reputation and a recommendation, or two, from someone whose opinion they trust. If you get your shot you want it to be good. A former student of mine moved to Los Angeles and relatively early on he received a call to do a film session. He is a great saxophonist, but at that time just a developing clarinetist. The call was for saxophone and clarinet. He showed up at the session but to his dismay the clarinet part was very difficult and exposed. The music for film sessions is generally unavailable in advance, since it is often written at the last minute. Calls for film dates go out a week or two ahead of the session, more or less. The service that puts out the call gives a reminder call and then finally an instrumentation call comes about 24 hours in advance of the session. If you're a woodwind player, you often won't know the exact instruments you will be playing until the instrumentation call, and you never know what will be in your part. It can be very easy or very scary. To add to the pressure, oftentimes you may have to play a cue 10 or more times because changes are being made on the fly. The challenge is to nail each take.

He made it through the session but it wasn't comfortable for him. He told me that he didn't hear from that contractor again for several years, and he presumed that it was because he didn't knock the ball out of the park on that first session. But that might not have been the case at all. Getting rehired is contingent on many things. Composers often request certain musicians, and contractors have their favorites and will try to use them exclusively. Then sometimes there are just lulls in the business and not much work is available. It is easy to feel like it is your fault when the phone doesn't ring, or when you hear that someone got a call you wanted, but don't let it get you down. Just keep moving ahead.

When I am hiring musicians that I don't know, I ask them if they feel confident about the gig that I am offering. If it's to play lead trumpet, or any of the jazz chairs in a big band, I want to make sure that I am getting players who will be in their element and do a good job. Just because someone is outstanding in one area doesn't guarantee that he or she will be in another. I remember one date when a well-known jazz drummer was hired (not by me) to play drum set in a studio orchestra setting. It was not good. The drummer was not that strong a reader and what he played didn't compliment the ensemble and make it easy to play. (A good drummer can improve the sight-reading of the group just by the way he or she sets up rhythmic passages.) In this case he was a great small group player, but that experience and expertise didn't translate to the more structured jazz orchestra setting. He felt bad and we felt bad for him.

Know How To Turn Down a Gig

When I'm hiring and make a call or send an email and get a slow response, I've found that, more often than not, the person will probably not take the job. If you know you are unavailable let the contractor know as soon as possible. Don't delay responding. He or she wants to get everything in place and the sooner the better. If you think you might be available but have to check on a commitment that was tentative, let the contractor know that you got his message and that you will check on things. Tell him or her that you will have an answer by a certain date or time. If you want to be considered for further gigs, be apologetic. I usually say something like this, "I'm sorry, I'd really like to do it, but I have to turn you down. I already have something on that date, but don't lose my file! Please think of me the next time."

It's Okay To Say "I Don't Know"

Some people, particularly those in authoritative positions like teachers and conductors, have a difficult time with this. None of us can know everything, even when it's in our area of specialization. It's not a sign of weakness to say, "I don't know," especially if you follow that by, "but I'll find out," or "but Bill can probably answer that." Bluffing your way through something that you aren't sure of lowers your overall credibility.

You Don't Have To Be Perfect All the Time

We're all human and by definition none of us are perfect, so it's okay to admit our mistakes. In my student days I remember playing under some conductors who when making a beat-pattern mistake, for example, would immediately correct a person or section in an effort to cover up their own screw up. We weren't that stupid. We knew what was going on. It's better to be humble and self-effacing than arrogant, if you want to have a good rapport with your colleagues.

Make Yourself Indispensible

In reality no one is indispensible. There is always someone out there to take your place. They might not fill your job exactly as you leave it, and there might be some scrambling and rough moments for a period of time, but things will eventually settle down and you will be a memory. With that said . . . your challenge is to do such a good job that your peers and superiors can't imagine anyone filling your shoes. Don't just do what is expected. Do *more* than is expected.

What Do You Do *Beyond* Your Job Description?

Over the years I've had dozens of graduate student assistants. Some have put in their time and have done what is expected, but others have gone above and beyond the call of duty. One student in particular comes to mind. This person was a jazz saxophone major whose duties were to teach private lessons to high school students in the Eastman Preparatory Department, college students from the University of Rochester (Eastman is a school within the University of Rochester) who weren't majoring in saxophone and Eastman music majors who were taking saxophone as a secondary instrument. With some of his high school students, Miles decided to form a saxophone quintet that primarily played jazz. He added a rhythm section and even had the students write and arrange some of the music for the group. He really motivated them and the group ended up winning a *Downbeat* magazine award. One of the students also won an individual award for best high school blues/pop/rock soloist.

Miles wasn't satisfied with just doing the gig. He saw an opportunity, recognized the talent of the students and guided them on to achievements that they had never dreamed they were capable of. Needless to say, Miles has gone on to be a very successful college teacher and performer . . . and that student who won the individual award? He also has a very good college teaching position.

Career or Job

I have a career as a teacher and professional musician, but my father had a job. It was definitely a job. He hated it. It was work. He was a glazier (a person who works with window glass and mirrors). What is the difference between the two, and do all musicians have careers as opposed to jobs? I started getting interested in this question, so I did what we do nowadays. I went to the web. There is an interesting site that compares, contrasts and states the difference between things— diffen.com/. I typed in "career vs. job" and found this.[42]

A career
- is the pursuit of a lifelong ambition or the general course of progression toward lifelong goals
- usually requires special training
- may not mean stability of work as it encourages one to take risks
- is generally long term

A job
- is an activity through which an individual can earn money. It is a regular activity in exchange for payment
- may or may not require education or special training
- is "safe" since there is job security and income
- is generally short term

So what's the answer? Do musicians have careers or jobs? I think it is up to the individual. Those of us in music full time begin with career aspirations. We pursue our lifelong goals. But some of us, particularly those who find themselves doing repetitive or routine work, can slip out of the career mindset. When music becomes a job it is time to rethink priorities and make adjustments. I can think of numerous examples of musicians in all areas of the business who have "checked out" and are just putting in their time. They are strictly coin-operated. This doesn't have to happen. To avoid this, a positive attitude is essential. When playing the same piece of music for the umpteenth time (read: *Nutcracker* or any Broadway show) try to find something new in it. Sure, it will seem like a job on some days, but when it starts feeling like that day after day, you won't be doing yourself or the music any good.

Know When To Fold 'Em

We've all probably seen athletes who try to compete when they are past their prime. Numerous examples immediately come to mind from football, baseball and boxing, just to name a few. As a kid my baseball hero was Mickey Mantle, a New York Yankees center fielder. He was at the top of his game in the 1950s. Toward the end of his career, in the late 60s, his legs were gone. He was moved to first base so he didn't have to run as much as in center field. His batting average slumped below 300. He was tired. He was clearly over the hill, but he kept on playing. It was sad to see a person who was once the best sink to mediocrity.

If you are a young musician the concept of when you will stop playing is not anywhere on your radar screen, but your day will come. Just like athletes, musicians lose some of their dexterity as they age. But the upside is that they have experience and familiarity with the music that they have spent a lifetime playing. In many genres of music, musicians continue playing into their 80s and even 90s, but with orchestra players, particularly wind, brass and principal strings, the pressure to remain in top form is great. They are also under a microscope most of the time. They have to sound good. In the 39 years or so that I have played in the Rochester Philharmonic Orchestra, I've witnessed a handful of musicians who should have retired, but like Mickey Mantle continued to come up to bat and would often strike out.

One incident many years ago really hit home for me. A young violinist, who was new to Rochester and the wife of one of my students, auditioned for and got on the sub list for the RPO. She played her first rehearsal and in a conversation with me I asked her how things were going and how she liked playing in the group. She said she enjoyed the orchestra very much and was having a good time. Then she asked me, "Who's the old guy on oboe?" I was taken aback. I revered that "old guy on oboe." Though oboe was not my primary instrument, I had had the honor of studying with him, and I found him to be one of the most insightful musicians and teachers with whom I had ever worked. My wife had also studied with him, played in his section and was like a daughter to him. But my young friend didn't have a background with "the old guy on oboe." To her the person she heard was just an old man who sometimes struggled to deliver.

That was a good lesson day for me. I learned two valuable things: First, people judge your playing and musicianship based on what they presently hear plus their history with you. Second, don't be like Mickey Mantle. Leave when you are still on top.

Always Remember Why You Decided on a Career in Music

Do you remember when you first decided on a life in music? It was pretty cool. You were full of energy and hope. But in the professional world, over time, "work" can grind you down and burn you out. Job dissatisfaction is certainly not exclusively limited to musicians, but this is a music book so I have to talk about it. In virtually all areas of the music business there are examples of musicians slogging their way through life just putting in their time. But perhaps the most infamous are orchestra musicians. They are notorious for complaining about most everything imaginable. Someone's chair is not right, the light is in their eyes, the conductor is inept, the person next to them has on too much perfume or aftershave, the music is boring, etc.

The key to a fulfilling life in music is to keep positive. If you find yourself getting down about your career, just think back to the time when you first decided to be a musician. It may give you a jumpstart and encourage you to explore new projects.

Keep Your Dream Alive

When your career starts to click, and it will if you hang in there, you may wake up one day and find yourself in a different place than you imagined. That can be good or it can be bad. Over the years many of my students have aspired to be jazz musicians, and so they have moved to New York or other big cities and hammered away trying to get noticed. Playing jazz is very personally rewarding, but the problem is that it is extremely difficult to make a living doing just that. As a result many jazz musicians, especially ones just starting out, take other kinds of work in order to put bread on the table. For them it can be possible to get caught up in making a living and lose track of why they went to New York in the first place.

As your career develops, doors of opportunity will be opened. Some of these opportunities will lead you to even more exciting and personally rewarding experiences that you could not have possibly imagined when you were young. But conversely some of these doors may lead to a dead end. It's the dead end that we want to avoid. The challenge is to recognize those dead ends for what they are. You want a career and not a job. Don't get stuck in a job. Keep your dream alive.

Being a Successful Entrepreneur

Don't Make Money the Number One Objective–Learn To Wait

Presumably you've chosen music because you love it and can't imagine yourself doing anything else. But, on the off chance that you are in music for the money, you've chosen the wrong profession. Sure, there are certain celebrity artists who make big, big money, but there is no doubt that the rank and file musician makes less money than the rank and file investment banker. Right out of college you probably won't be buying that BMW.

Money can be a bad motivator for us if it takes precedence over our artistic standards. It has the potential to cause us to shift our focus off of quality and to take gigs just for the money. Good motivators, like developing a more secure technique or gaining a deeper understanding of the music we play, raise our level of musicianship. If you build your house on solid ground and put it up brick by brick, financial rewards will come. You will be noticed and people will be willing to pay you well for what you do. Careers are built over time. Of course certain events can occur that will catapult you forward or raise you to another level. You might get a new, more prestigious job or some of your works published, but by and large, after you have reached a level of excellence on your instrument, success in music is achieved by slow and steady work as you acquire knowledge and experience.

Don't Dilute Your Product in Order To Make Money

I once had a conversation with Maria Schneider in which she made an interesting observation: many musicians who are focused solely on making money underestimate their audiences. She commented that some musicians seem to think that if they write or present a particular kind of music, they will get a certain audience. A dilemma can occur if they happen to get lucky and are successful in gaining an audience. If they suddenly say "that's not really who I am." "Let me show you what I really do," they will lose that audience, because those fans were on board for what the artist was doing at the time. They came to the concert just for that.

Of utmost importance is to be devoted to developing your own craft and your own voice. If you follow your artistic calling with passion and belief, when your audience does find you, they will be getting the best of what you have to offer. Be true to yourself. Don't pander.

Don't Be Embarrassed about Making Money

In talking with Maria further, she had an interesting take on the stereotypical starving artist. She theorizes that part of the reason record companies are able to make huge profits while the artists often make so little is because many musicians have the idea that being a starving artist somehow raises the value of their art. Some have the attitude that commercial success equates to selling out, and the minute something is popular it's devalued. This becomes a "badge of honor" that some artists like to wear. That attitude has played right into the hands of the business world. Think about other occupations or professions. Can you imagine a baker saying, "I don't really want to make money selling my cakes. I do it because I just love to see people appreciate how good my food is. I don't care if I lose money"? Nobody would ever do that in any business other than the arts! The business world says, "Wow, we've got this commodity here, and we don't have to pay much for it. And as a matter of fact, they are happier if we don't pay them for it!" This may be a little extreme, but you get the point.

Maria goes on to say that it's important to instill in people the idea that it's possible to do incredible high-value work and be paid for it. Music shouldn't be free. Yes, as musicians we are smart and lucky. We do what we love and get paid for it. It shouldn't mean that because we love doing what we do we should do it for free. We work very hard and we should be paid well for it.

There Is No One Model for Entrepreneurs–Gain Experience First

Think back to Chapter 9: "Five Non-Linear Career Journeys." These are stories of very successful entrepreneurial musicians. I chose to include them because they represent five different areas of the music business, but I had a secondary reason as well. They all have reached their goals in different ways. There really is no single road to success in music. If you gain experience, be observant, have good role models and develop an entrepreneurial mindset, your time will come.

Once a friend of a friend asked me what her daughter could do to prepare for a career in music. Her daughter was then a high school student and was considering a college major in music. Half-jokingly I gave her a flip answer. I said, "Tell her she should 1) get a paper route, because then she will know how many papers she has to deliver just to purchase one CD; and 2) get a ukulele, because she will learn how to harmonize tunes with just three chords." In other words, know the value of a dollar and work on your ears. But, something was lost in my profundity: I forgot that kids haven't had paper routes in 30 years. Got to change that one.

Envision the Future

When I was a doctoral student, I was in a class that had an assignment that asked us to think into the future 20 years and forecast what the music profession would look like. I wish I still had that paper. It would be fun to see how far off I was. Anyway, one student was very frustrated with the assignment. She just couldn't get into it. I remember one of her comments. "What should we do? Take LSD to help stimulate our imaginations?" Okay, it was the '60s. But talk about inside-the-box thinking! She was all about what was going on in the present and pretty short on imagination!

That student not withstanding, it's kind of fun to think about future trends. Here is a thought I had just today. I have a student who is finishing his doctorate in jazz studies, and he is writing a dissertation. I'm not his primary advisor, but I'm on his committee and so I have to read this document, make comments and edits and when it is in good shape I'll sign off on it. There are three of us on his committee. As I read his dissertation today I thought, "The content is great, but the delivery system is very antiquated. It has a footnote about every other sentence, and because it is about music it has tons of musical examples." I'm thinking that this is the same format as 40 years ago when I went through the identical process with my dissertation. Why can't this be done in an electronic format with links to the footnotes and embedded musical examples? It would be so much more user-friendly. The reader could hear the examples while looking at the music. I know that the technology is there. In our website, polyphonic.org, we embedded sound files in one of our articles two years ago.[43] Maybe there is no need to do this for a dissertation (if you assume that it will never be read again except by a handful of scholars), but I will wager that 10 years from now more books will be published in electronic format than hard copy, and that they will have all sorts of interactive add-ons available. The publishing industry is already firmly headed in this direction.

In envisioning the future, I am reminded of this quote that is attributed to hockey legend Wayne Gretzky. It's a good one. When asked how he always seemed to be in the right place at the right time, and consequently scored more goals than others, he replied, "I don't go where the puck is. I go to where the puck will be." Try to be like Gretzky.

Think Big–or Go Home

When I was younger I'm sure I didn't think "Big Picture" as much as I do now, but today with countless projects under my belt, I'm always thinking big. I suppose it's also a function of my job at the Eastman School. As a senior administrator and Director of the Institute for Music Leadership, it's my job to be forward thinking.

I've found that a successful way to approach any project, or problem for that matter, is to dream about what it could be if there were no constraints on resources, i.e., money and staff to make it happen (read: the "staff" is sometimes just me!). When working with others I try to neutralize the naysayers right away. It's very easy to throw cold water on an idea at the outset. I try to have everyone think of all the positive things about the project. After we have considered those, I ask for challenges or barriers to the idea. There are usually workarounds for the barriers. As suggested elsewhere in this book, envision the Cadillac version. Put some numbers to it, then start making compromises if you need to. This is what orchestra artistic administrators do in planning a season. They come up with interesting concerts, but then the reality of the budget sets in. How many extra players are going to be needed? Leos Janácek's *Sinfonietta* might look great programmatically, but with its large instrumentation and many extra players—including twelve trumpets, two bass trumpets, four trombones, two tenor tubas and one tuba—it just might stretch the budget a little.

Think Global

As my students ponder their futures in music, I always advise them to think beyond their hometowns, their states, their regions and countries. Today especially, the opportunities are worldwide, and the good news is that we can find out about them through the Internet and online courses. Musicians with skills in a second or third language can uncover opportunities that are otherwise closed.

One summer I had an opportunity to teach a two-week workshop at a jazz school in France. I knew that, in general, the French don't embrace the study of English like many of the other European countries do, and that I would have to be able to communicate somewhat in that language. I had French in high school, but didn't do well in it. Nevertheless, I got some tapes and started a self-study program. By the time the workshop rolled around I had some basics going. All things considered, I actually did fairly well by using musical terms, demonstrating on my instrument and speaking my fractured French. But when they asked me back for the following year, I decided to kick it up a notch. I got a tutor who came to my office once a week. She gave me the usual lessons, but also personalized it for me. I needed to know the words for things like: music stand, start from the beginning, whole note, quarter note, etc. I had homework, but since I was motivated and into it, it was fun. I returned the second year and this time I was also adjudicating some final exams. The grammar wasn't always there, but I was able to write my comments in French and I felt very good about that. With my improved language skills I could also connect better with the students.

Still another opportunity came the next year. I was invited by Jean-Marie Londeix, with whom I had studied in Nice one summer, to present a paper and play at the 150th year celebration of the invention of the saxophone. There was going to be simultaneous translation from French to English and English to French, but I decided to deliver my paper in French. I wrote it out in English, translated it into French, and with the aid of my teacher took out or changed any words that if mispronounced would be totally stupid or off-color. (I gave my teacher a huge tip for thinking of that little detail!) She recorded it for me, so I studied by listening to her pronunciation and reading the text.

The big day finally came. Everyone filed into the auditorium and picked up their headsets, as they always do when guests from other countries speak. I boldly began to deliver my paper in French, saying how happy I was to be in Angers and the Loire valley, and what a good conference it had been so far. I started hearing *click, click . . . click-click*. They were turning off their headsets! They understood me! I finished my twenty-minute paper, then performed, "Sonata for Soprano Saxophone and Piano" written by my colleague Bill Dobbins who also presented a paper in French that day (Bill is fluent in French as well as German, but that's another story).

From that point on we were in. At lunch we would eat with the French guys. We really connected with them. It was so much more meaningful to be in a foreign country and hanging with the natives rather than with the Americans. After all, we could experience them anytime. I continued my studies with my French tutor, which evolved into private lessons with her for two-and-a-half years. I also established a relationship with a French publisher, Alphonse Leduc, who published four of my saxophone etude books.

Language can be another element that separates you from the pack, especially in today's global economy. Keep your mind open and look for opportunities anywhere and everywhere.

Big Problem = Big Opportunity

Think about it. For every problem there is an opportunity for someone who can offer a solution. But, as President Obama said when speaking about the economic condition in 2009, "Solving a big problem is not easy. If it was, it would have already been done." Every day each of us is confronted with problems, or challenges as they say. Don't shy away from them. Think creatively, and in addition to looking for answers in your usual way, look for solutions that may not be so straight-line.

Think back to Chapter 9 and the Todd and Chandra story. They had a problem. They were in Japan and Chandra's job was coming to a close. As they lived in their town and learned more about it, they observed that private teaching of band instruments was virtually nonexistent. That market seemed wide open to them, but they had to create a demand for it. They did that by producing concerts and gaining a reputation of excellence.

Don't Spend a Lot of Time Looking in Your Rear-View Mirror

In life all of us will make some mistakes. We won't win every audition, get every job for which we apply or for that matter play up to our personal expectations in every performance. Successful performers learn to recover quickly from their missteps. They recover and go on. Experience has shown them that if they let a small bobble bother them, they run the risk of losing confidence and destroying an entire passage. Just as we learn to recover in performance, we must transfer that ability to life. Mistakes will happen. Learn from them, but don't dwell on them. What's done is done, so look to the future by keeping focused on your goals.

Don't Confuse Entrepreneurship with Self-Promotion or Making Something

I've often observed that musicians can get hung up on the word "entrepreneur." To an idealistic person it may seem antithetical to the arts. I think that some "artists" often confuse entrepreneurship with self-promotion, or they equate it with inventing or making something. Remember our definition of entrepreneurship—**the transformation of an idea into an enterprise that creates value**. For us it is not necessarily about creating a new and different percussion mallet, an improved trumpet mute or a perfect plastic reed. In reality most musicians have entrepreneurial projects. When I look at the Eastman faculty I see a violin professor who runs his summer string quartet program, a pianist who hosts an international piano competition, an organ department that is creating an organ Mecca in Rochester, a jazz faculty that is all over the U.S. and Europe playing their music and historians and theorists writing and promoting their latest books. The list goes on. It's what we do. We create. And anything worth doing is worth sharing with others. Someone willing to pay us for this talent makes it so much the better. As long as strong playing and solid musicianship back up the entrepreneurial aspect of your musical life, no one will call you a self-promoter.

Running a Successful Business–You, Inc.

Act Like a Business

You, Inc. is a business, so you need to act like one. You should look as professional as possible. This includes everything from business cards to websites. I was just out of college and someone recommended me to do a little arrangement of a pop song. Not only did I have to arrange it for two or three horns, I also had to transcribe it from a recording. The composer was what is known in the jingle world as "a hummer." But that's another chapter in itself—people who "write songs" but don't read, write or for that matter play music. Anyway, I did the job. We recorded it and everyone was happy, so the composer asked me to send him a bill—an invoice. I went to music school. I didn't remember the subject of "invoicing the client" in my 8:00 A.M. theory class. The point is, in business, when services have been rendered, you bill them. This provides a written record of the job and allows your client to pay you. It also helps you keep your records straight. An invoice doesn't have to be elaborate, but it's something You, Inc. will need.

Clients like to feel confident that you know what you are doing. When I first began doing radio and television contracting for national accounts, I immediately contacted the union and became signatory[44] to every agreement that I could. If I was going to operate in that arena I had to know, or have access to, the rules.

One more thing: now that you're a professional get rid of that email address that seemed so clever in high school. Your *PookeyPuppy* handle doesn't make it anymore. The same is true for the greeting on your answering machine. Your precocious daughter singing Old MacDonald doesn't cut it. Make sure the photos that strangers can access on any social network to which you may belong are not questionable. Use common sense and remember your brand. Protect it—and yourself.

Do Things When You Say You Will

You have to meet deadlines. If you tell someone you will get back to them by Thursday, you have to get back to them by Thursday (and

Wednesday would be better). People really appreciate being taken care of promptly. If you tell a contractor you have to check on the date and that you'll be back to him tomorrow, it better be tomorrow, because a slow response from you may create a problem for him. Often a contractor just wants an answer from you. If it's no, that's okay. He can then move on to another person. But a slow response just keeps him in limbo for a while. Of course, if you are a composer it is obvious that you have to meet deadlines. If you miss one it can set off a chain reaction that affects others down the line. But occasionally there are extenuating circumstances that slow you down, and in those cases you can renegotiate a later deadline. But you'd better make that second one.

Dress the Part

In the business world a person's work clothes will most likely be a suit or sport coat, white shirt and tie for men or a suit (pants or skirt) for women. In the arts, the business dress code is all over the place. I'm sure the Rolling Stones do not put on a suit and tie to talk to record company executives, but if you are applying for a teaching job, a loan from a bank or going to court for any reason, it's probably a good idea to try to look like the people you are trying to impress. In my years as a saxophone professor at Eastman, I've listened to a lot of juries (yearly playing exams), and invariably there will be negative comments among the committee if a person looks like he just changed the oil in his car.

Talk Less–Listen and Observe

If you are new in a band, orchestra, school faculty or practically any group, it is probably best to get the "lay of the land" before launching into your political or religious views. Find out who are the leaders and stay away from the bitter, burned-out negative folks. Groups develop cultures and ways of interacting with each other, and if you inadvertently violate one of their unwritten "laws" you can get off to a rocky start with them. Here is an example.

A friend of mine was playing saxophone with the New York City Ballet. As a saxophonist he was probably just playing one piece and he certainly wasn't a regular member of the group, but the number of performances was going to be substantial. On one occasion during the rehearsals my friend needed to have a substitute. He asked and received permission to send a sub that happened to be a mutual friend of ours. When my friend showed up at the next rehearsal he asked the contractor how things went. The contractor said that the sub played fine but don't use him again! My friend asked why, and the contractor said that during the break the sub practiced jazz licks very loudly—lots of notes and noise.

A few things went wrong here. First, breaks are breaks. Picture in your mind this person playing very loud jazz licks on the saxophone when the rest of the group is talking about their families or their next vacation. Students continue to practice or in many cases mindlessly play during a break. You don't hear that with professionals. Someone may be checking a reed for a minute or two or a new violin, but you don't have the cacophony that you find in student groups. Second, you should warm up on the music or style that you are going to play in the rehearsal. That means leave the jazz licks at home if you get an orchestra call, and finally, if you are a saxophonist you are already an odd duck in an orchestra. Blend in. Our friend forgot to listen and observe and that first impression cost him, though he probably never realized it. He just didn't get called back.

Discipline Yourself

Though the music business encompasses a vast number of individuals, each subset has it's own "membership" and the musicians within that subset know each other or are certainly familiar with each other, if only by reputation. Let's think about orchestra players, and we'll use the flute as an example. The musicians in the 50 largest orchestras in the U.S. belong to an organization called the International Conference of Symphony and Opera Musicians (ICSOM). There are no more than 200 flutists who belong to this ICSOM "club." Predictably, there is a flute grapevine. They go to flute conventions and read about each other in publications. It's the same for Broadway players, country or LA studio musicians—you name it. There is an *unofficial* communication network in each of these sub-groups. For this reason it is extremely important that you be disciplined and respectful of your peers. If you bad-mouth someone it always has a way of getting back to that person. This is fine, I suppose, if you want to send a message, but if you don't you had better be disciplined and keep your mouth shut. My New York friends really know this. They are always very respectful of their peers. On the surface everyone is a great guy and has something musical to offer. You have to drill down a bit to find out what they really think.

Be Diplomatic

Because of these individual subsets within the music world—i.e., your instrument, styles of music associated with you, the city in which you live and so on—your musical world is smaller than you think. This requires that you be diplomatic and discreet in your professional dealings.

In Rochester, New York, where the Eastman School of Music is located and where I live, there was, in the '80s and '90s, an active recording scene. The business in town was local as well as national and was generated primarily by three producers who each had their areas of specialization and their own clients, but from time to time there would be overlap. I was fortunate to be the contractor for all three. It was only natural that each had an interest in what the other was doing and often at sessions I would hear something like the following: "I hear you were in last week doing a session for Mr. X, how did it go?" In other words, how big was the session? Who was the client? What was the music? Who did the arrangements? Was it good? Was the client pleased? And so on. I had to be very discreet, because even though they had carved out their own piece of the action, they still felt in competition with each other. In my conversations with them I made sure not to be derogatory. We all know the guy who puts everyone down to the point where you wonder what he says about you when you aren't around. I didn't want to be that person! I had to be positive about the session, but not effusive. I had to walk a fine line. They had to know that I would not shoot off my mouth about their sessions. I had to be discreet. In a word, I had to be professional. It seemed to work. I still do sessions for them today, though not nearly as many as in the heyday.

Be Objective When it Matters

In times of tough decisions it is especially important to be able to separate the issues from the personalities, to be detached, to be objective by stepping back and removing yourself from the mix. This happens all the time if you are a teacher or a contractor. You can hire your friends if they can deliver the goods, but if they slip it's your reputation that is on the line. Friendship can break a tie between hiring one person over another, but it can't be the only reason you hire someone.

As a teacher it is quite natural to become very attached to your students. But there are times when one of your favorites has screwed up and now must suffer the consequences. I can remember several times when I had to give a student a bad grade or tell him that he had just failed his doctoral oral exam. The students certainly didn't want to hear the message I was delivering, but they accepted it and came back for a second attempt, this time, well prepared. One particular student, who passed on the second go-round, thanked me for making him repeat it saying that now he could really feel good about getting the degree.

Don't Burn Bridges

It is always best to leave a position on a positive note even if there has been turmoil leading up to your departure, because you never know when you might have to return looking for work. An orchestra friend of mine told me of one incident when one of the players in his orchestra won a major position in a Big Five orchestra. She couldn't immediately take the job, so there was a period of time when she was playing out her present contract while waiting to go to her new job. During this period her attitude changed, and she could often be heard bad-mouthing her old job and some of her colleagues. She moved on to her new job, but when her tenure review came up it was denied. She was out of work. It just so happened that her old job simultaneously became available. She thought she could easily get it back, but the player's committee, I'm sure remembering her "scorched earth" exit, required her to take an audition. It wasn't surprising that she went nowhere and didn't even make the finals. This is a good illustration of how small the music world can be. It might momentarily feel good to give them a piece of your mind when you think you have nothing to lose, but you never know when you might be back knocking on their door looking for work. Be cool.

Ask for Advice–Have a Mentor, Have a Confidant

We can't go it alone. All of us need someone we trust and respect to give us a reality check once in a while. This person can be a peer, a former teacher, an older colleague; you may even have more than one person, depending on the subject under discussion. My *consigliere* (if you've seen the Godfather movies you will recognize that word) is a good friend of 40 years. I often test my ideas on him or get his opinion on personal or professional issues that I might be facing, and he does the same with me. As a teacher at Eastman I had two older, wiser professors who took me under their wings. There was nothing official between us. They were just interested in me and wanted me to succeed. And now that I am more senior at Eastman, I am often asked for advice and guidance from less experienced faculty members. I even have my home repair mentor. Every homeowner needs a neighbor who can fix just about anything!

Ask for advice. It's not a sign of weakness. I remember one new junior faculty hire who got off to a bad start, didn't ask for advice from anyone, didn't make friends with faculty, didn't get good mentoring from the department chair and more or less tried to go it alone. He did some dumb things that could have been averted if he would have just reached out and asked for counsel from someone who had been around. He had good things to offer, but, not surprisingly, he wasn't renewed. But importantly, when you *do* get advice from someone you trust, *listen* to it.

Mean What You Say

Picture this scenario. You're in a restaurant. A family is seated nearby. The dining experience doesn't seem to be going too well for everyone. You hear the mother tell the youngest child to clean up her plate, and if she doesn't she will get no dessert. The child resists, gets fidgety and starts to act up. The mother, wanting to avoid a showdown, softens her position a little. "You don't have to eat the vegetables, just eat the meat and potatoes." The child escalates the conflict, now crying and saying she won't do it. Other customers begin to look over to see what the ruckus is. The mother says, "Just drink your milk and you'll get dessert." The kid happily drinks her milk and gets the dessert. This parent didn't mean what she said and the child knew it. The child got her way.

This also happens in real life among adults. I wish I had just one dollar for every time I have heard, "I'm sorry it can't be more money this time, but I have a lot of other things coming up. Just work with me this once. I'll give you a call." After a while you know who these people are—the ones with big promises and no delivery. They lose credibility as soon as those predictable words are uttered. If you say something, mean it.

Do Something Nice

We had to put our fourteen-year-old Rhodesian Ridgeback down last week—old age. He just couldn't do it anymore. Out of the blue the vet sent us a condolence card signed by him and his entire staff. That was an unexpected, kind gesture. Do you think I will continue taking my animals to this vet? I sure will! Little things like thank you or sympathy cards or congratulatory phone calls for jobs well done can really mean a lot. It shows you care about the person. Could I do more of this? Sure. We all could.

A friend of mine relayed a telling story to me. She was talking to her friend who is a recruiter for a large software company. He told her that at a recent job fair, he received more than 500 résumés for one particular job. "How did you narrow that number down to a manageable few," she asked. "It was easy," he said. "I just looked at the ones who sent me a thank you!" (There were seven.)

Let People Off the Hook

A deal is a deal, but . . . I always let people off the hook. Will I remember the incident and consider it when thinking of hiring them again in the future? Absolutely! Will it be a positive or negative feeling? It depends.

Occasionally, I will have someone booked for a gig who will come to me with a conflict. It could be a personal issue or they may have been offered another job that they would like to play, and they want to get out of my job. They tell me the details and nine times out of ten it will be a better opportunity for them—lots more money or better for them career wise. If we have worked together a lot and we know each other well, they know not to ask me unless it is better for them. So, I'm happy to let them take the other gig. But sometimes a student type will want to get out of gig just to make an extra $25. I always say yes, but they probably won't work for me for a long time. It is important to honor your commitments. Think about the future and don't make decisions based on short-term needs. That extra $25 may seem important at the time, but it could cost you lots more down the road. Many times I have had to turn down very good paying gigs because I was already committed. It happens.

If you do have a conflict, go to the person who hired you with a solution. Provide the names and contact information of substitutes who are right for the particular job. In fact, if you can call a likely sub and find out if they are available, that's even better. If you have a solution to the problem, the contractor will be very grateful, but if you leave him high and dry he will remember it.

Drive a Soft Bargain

To drive a hard bargain is, of course, to be demanding and unwilling to give ground when negotiating something. More often than not it is better to do the opposite and "drive a soft bargain." I practically gave away the first arrangement I did for an orchestra. I didn't have any real experience writing for that ensemble. I had done a couple of studio orchestra compositions, but I relied on the rhythm section and improvising soloists to carry the ball. When I got a call to do my first orchestra arrangement they were taking a chance on me, though they weren't aware of it. I was happy just to get my foot in the door, and it worked out well. I ended up doing several arrangements for them, which lead to others, and those to others and those. . . .

Always keep the big picture in mind. Don't try to make a killing on every opportunity. Build your reputation and lay some groundwork. Remember Jeff Tyzik's story in Chapter 9? When he was ready to take that step into the Pops conductor world, he gave them a price that was well below market. The orchestra figured they had nothing to lose. They had no ideas! He did, plus, he was cheap. Don't be shortsighted. (P.S.: That was then. This is now. Jeff is no longer cheap.)

Be Proactive Not Reactive

Just this past year a journalist was doing an article on musicians as entrepreneurs in *Inside Higher Ed*, an online source for news, jobs and opinion concerning higher education. The article was a good one and very positive. I was quoted several times, but one particular quote that was attributed to me went something like this, "You can't make a living playing piano." Gasp! Even if I thought that I would never say it! Somehow, I was misquoted. When I read this I had a sinking feeling in my stomach. To make matters worse, there had been a written communication that went to the entire Eastman community that told about the article, that Eastman was mentioned and of course, that I was quoted. I could picture my colleagues reading this and immediately starting to heat up the tar and pluck the chickens. What was I going to do? One option was to not do anything and hope that my colleagues wouldn't see it. I knew that tactic sometimes worked for politicians. But I figured that if even one of my colleagues picked up on this and told someone else, pretty soon there would be a buzz going on in the school. I decided to play offense and not defense. I sent an email to the entire school that explained that I was misquoted. I waited for the fallout, but there was none. I got some kidding from some of my friends, and one or two pianists even chimed in. I can't attribute the lack of negative response to the email that I wrote, but I sure felt better doing something instead of waiting to get some flack.

I like to put out fires before they get big and out of control. If you can sense a potential conflict brewing it's a good idea to address it head on. Open up a conversation. With good communication most disagreements are really misunderstandings. Get your cards on the table and settle things. For me it is better to act rather than react.

Know How To Get Lucky

Knowing how to get *lucky* seems like an oxymoron, but I do have a reason to say it that way. But before I tell you that, I have to tell you a story. I was once on an adjudication panel for a grant called the Creative Artist Public Service Grant. It doesn't exist today, but it funded New York State composers of all genres of music. The music submitted ran the gamut from established "classical" mainstream composers to experimentalists who dropped microphones into the New York harbor and made music from the recorded sounds. It also included all styles of jazz and folk music too. I suppose I was the jazz person on the panel. There were about 1,000 applications, but the foundation's staff had made a preliminary cut and only roughly 200 applications remained to be reviewed. From that group we were to select the 15 or 20 who would receive funding.

So there we were—five judges, the foundation's music administrator and a couple of helpers who shuttled scores back and forth and cued up tapes. This was still in the days of reel-to-reel tape and early cassettes. We were there for three days, and they were long ones—eight to ten hour days. Somewhere in the afternoon of the first day I looked around at my colleagues and saw how tired they were. They were burned out already. I then began to notice what grabbed their attention and what didn't. First, I observed that if they weren't immediately engaged with the music, they tuned it out. The pieces that were selected to go into the "review again later pile," as opposed to the ones that were discarded, were the ones that were immediately impressive. Second, the music had to be neat and easy to read. The tapes had to have leader between selections (old technology) and counter numbers on the scores for easier locating of sections. I remember one of the applications said something like this, "If time is of the essence, I would like you to be sure to hear the development section of my piece. Please scroll to counter number 265. That corresponds to measure 96 in the score." He was making our job easier for us! And finally, I also noticed that, at least with this panel, they seemed to be impressed if the composer was also playing or conducting on the recording. Three days later we picked our winners and I went back to Rochester with tinnitus.

The next year I applied for a CAPS grant. Guess what? I took my experience from the previous year and put together a recording that was immediately impressive. I made it very easy for them. I laid it out with neat and clear scores. I even used the, "If time is limited please go to counter number . . ." It worked. I got a CAPS grant. That, to me, is knowing how to get lucky.

Make a Pledge to Quality

There is no arguing with quality. If something is really good it doesn't have to be dressed up very much for people to recognize its value. Whatever you undertake try to take it to the max. If you keep high-level musicianship always in the forefront and entrepreneurship supporting it, you will find success and a fulfilling life in music.

Don't Be in a Hurry

I have a good time joking with my students and often when they become impatient with their progress and development on their instrument, I reassure them that they will get there. It's like baking a cake, I say. "We've got the ingredients, but you haven't been in the oven long enough. You're still a little soft in the middle." We want things now—immediate results and gratification. But some things just take time. Try to see the small improvements. When you leave your practice room at the end of the day, go over in your mind all the things that improved in that session and plan out what your course of action will be tomorrow.

Grow Slowly

If you follow business news at all, you can probably recount stories of companies that have tremendous growth and expansion only to get ahead of themselves and have to lay off workers when the demand for their product lessens. Think back to the clarinetist as small business metaphor in Chapter 1. If the clarinetist wants to expand his business (for example, seriously study the bass clarinet) and does so before his core business (playing the clarinet) is solid, there is a great risk that his clarinet playing will suffer. When you add a new product to your store, you must keep the quality of your core business at a high level. The more products you add, the more difficult this becomes. Have you ever seen a juggler who spins plates on thin poles? He starts off with three and everything is fine. He keeps adding plates one at a time, until he has seven or eight going at once, but there is always one that is ready to come crashing down. In your own career, when you're thinking of adding another plate, make sure the previous ones are spinning perfectly.

Diversify

At the outset, as you build your business (You, Inc.), most of the growth will center on your instrument. You will expand your repertoire. You'll add to the solo pieces that you have played in your college recitals and start including more chamber music (Legos). If you want to pursue an orchestra career you will begin hammering out those excerpts and getting them down cold (Legos). If your focus is jazz or commercial music you will be learning tunes (Legos) and trying to play with as many different people as you can. At some point your interests may lead you into an area that is away from your instrument. It may be composing like Jeff Tyzik, inventing things like Robert DiLutis or taking on administrative work, like running a music school, like Todd and Chandra. Who knows?

Several years ago I had a student, Aaron, whose father, a physicist, had a hobby making clay pots and other such objects. He and his wife would sell their wares at craft shows. They had all the equipment, and Aaron, from a very young age, was around this stuff all the time, so it was natural that he would dabble in this too. He made sculptures out of clay and even made a few conical bore instruments that played with a regular saxophone mouthpiece. Not really understanding acoustics at that age, the instruments just played some very odd-sounding scales. Anyway, it planted a seed in him. Curiosity brought him back to exploring the use of ceramics later on in life.

While he was a student at Eastman he started making clay flutes. He modeled them after bamboo flutes to get the basics of tone production, but they weren't the usual pentatonic ones. He made them with more interesting scales for jazz players—octatonic, harmonic minor. He also experimented with end-blown flutes, like the *quena*, which is the traditional flute of the Andes and *shakuhachi* from Japan, as well as fipple flutes like the recorder and penny whistle. He even experimented with double and triple fipple type flutes. These were folk instruments and he was able to place them in a catalogue called *The Music Stand*. (This was before the days of purchasing items over the Internet.) He did pretty well, and many people bought them, I'm sure, just to put in a display case. They looked very good.

Fast forward and now he's out of college. His interests and curiosity had taken him from clay flutes to making ceramic saxophone mouthpieces. I won't go into a discussion of the use of ceramic material in mouthpiece making, except to say that nobody was, or is, doing it except Aaron. With mouthpieces you really have to know what you are doing. Measurements and tolerances have to be exact. He's added other ceramic products for musicians, and this has turned into a business for him.[45] In addition to the business he continues to play and to teach.

Not only is this a story of diversification, it also illustrates how one thing can lead to the next. The progression could have been something like this:

- I think I'll make a pot.
- Pots are nice, but I play music. How about a flute?
- These flutes are boring. I wonder if I could make one with a more exotic scale or put a saxophone mouthpiece on them.
- Ceramics have all different kinds of applications. I'll try making a saxophone mouthpiece.

- They work! How about clarinet barrels, tuning rings, brass mouthpiece overlays?
- I wonder if . . .

Seek Out the Best To Teach You What You Don't Know

Presumably, if you are still in school you are currently doing this, but it doesn't mean you have to go to Harvard, MIT, Eastman or Juilliard. I went to the University of Denver for my bachelor's degree. It was perfect for me at the time. Hopefully from your formal schooling you will have discovered how to be your own teacher. Learning opportunities are everywhere. If you have a chamber group, you can learn from each other. If you are a young jazz musician and you get a gig, try to hire more experienced players than you. Surround yourself with others who are higher up on the food chain. Play with the big boys whenever you can. Certainly if you have a business and employees or if you run a department or division in a company or school, you will want to hire others who can guide you and fill in gaps in your own expertise. You don't have to be the smartest guy in the room. Surround yourself with smart, talented people. They will teach you what you don't know.

Know What You Don't Know

Along with seeking out the best to teach you, it is absolutely necessary to know what you don't know. You've probably met a few individuals who think they have it all together, have everything under control, and know exactly what they are doing—but in actuality they are clueless. The frustrating part is that they don't recognize this!

A student came to his lesson one day. He was a freshman or sophomore and a talented jazz saxophonist. He told me he was called to play a production of *West Side Story* with a local high school. They had hired a few "ringers" to beef up the pit orchestra. But he was hired to play the clarinet book! You can't have just "messed around" on this instrument. You have to be a clarinetist to play this book. It calls for E-flat, B-flat and bass clarinets. This student was talented, but there was no way he could come close to cutting the part. I told him this, but he was more or less oblivious. He truly didn't know what he didn't know. I forgot to add that this student thought very highly of himself. He was good, but not as good as he thought. Maybe that's part of the problem with these personality types. I won't give you the details on how the gig finally played out, but he should have listened to my advice.

Be Flexible

The first time I did a project in a foreign country I learned how to roll with the punches. But when I did the second one, I got my graduate degree in "don't worry—be happy." I really learned how to be flexible. It was France. There were so many curveballs. It seemed like everything got changed. Even on the flight over, it still wasn't clear to me exactly what we were going to be doing. I knew that we were going to teach, play a few concerts and make a CD, but that was about it. Our hosts had assembled several American musicians and together with French musicians we made up a big band. The compositions and arrangements were by French and U.S. composers. The teaching part was first and that went fine. We were also rehearsing during the nights because we were going to do a day-long recording session on a Sunday, then the following week play three or four gigs around the area. Now, the usual sequence would be, rehearse, play some concerts, *then* record. But for whatever reason the recording was first.

Sunday came. The session wasn't in a studio. It was in a small auditorium that had a stage, and the recording gear was brought in just for this date. The saxophone section, being good boy scouts, arrived to have a sectional at what we thought was two hours early. We were ready. The session starting time came, and we were joined by one lonesome trombone. Did we get the time wrong? The band began dribbling in, but it wasn't fully assembled until at least two hours after the start time. But we were all there now.

We finally got going. It sounded terrible. Nothing was going right. A trombonist, I think the one who was actually on time, stood up with his tuner in his hand. *"Trente-neuf! Trente-neuf!"* (thirty-nine) he shouted. The piano was out of tune. It was flat, and instead of being tuned to

A=440 or slightly above, it had slipped to A=439. Oh, someone forgot to have the piano tuned! Oh well! The session slammed to a halt, and a piano technician was called. Luckily he could come right over. We worked on a few more things without the piano, but when the technician arrived we all went across the street to the café. (It is very dangerous for French musicians to get near food and drink, when they still have a job to do.) We all had a beer and then sent one of our comrades back to check on the status of the piano tuning. He returned and said, "He's really into it. The piano is torn apart." Too bad. So we decided to eat! Now we were really in trouble, because the French don't just wolf down a Big Mac. They dine.

Long story short—a couple of hours later, well fed and feeling very good from the wine, we straggled back. We continued to record, but didn't get anything down that was useable. We looked at the clock. The saxes had been there 12 hours. We went to plan B. On the following day we were to play a concert in the same hall. We asked the engineers if they were available to record and they were, so our hosts decided that we would make it a live recording. The plan was that we would see how the concert went, then afterward we would re-record anything that needed touching up.

Another long story short—the concert was okay, but not stellar. We ended up staying past midnight, just re-recording some of the pieces—then someone had an idea. We had two or three more concerts booked that week, so the engineers were asked if they could come along with us and record them. They could. We eventually ended up with a good product, but not without an inordinate amount of adjusting on everyone's part.

In situations like these it is easy for everyone to get pumped up and start screaming at each other. In these circumstances I just go with the flow. I didn't plan it. It's not my gig. I can't control it. They've got me for a couple of weeks. I'm at their service. This story is an extreme example, but the fact is that not everything goes as planned. Things happen. There can be equipment problems that cause musicians to stay longer than contracted, or something can happen to cause the rehearsal to start late.

Orchestra musicians are notorious for clock watching. When the big hand gets to 12, the rehearsal is over. In the commercial world the clock is not taken so literally. Leaders, producers, and contractors very much appreciate musicians who are flexible and can "play ball" when necessary. These overtime situations make a contractor's life miserable. They have to straddle the fence, representing the musicians' interests, but keeping the producers, whose money is on the line, happy. Five or ten minutes overtime shouldn't be that much of an inconvenience to the majority of the players, and if it saves the producer $500+ it's good to be flexible and not make it an issue.

Know Your Competition

Companies keep up to date on their competitors' new products. They are keenly aware of their competition, and some even go through the process of reverse engineering (read: taking apart) a product to discover their rivals' secrets. Think about the musicians in your town who are doing the kind of work that you want to do. What is it about them that makes them desirable? What are their strengths? How do you stack up against them? What can you take from their "playbook" and incorporate into your own playing?

As musicians we can do our own version of reverse engineering. Listen to one of your favorite performers. Don't just listen casually. Really get down and analyze his or her sound and phrasing. Students of jazz do this all the time. In learning to play jazz, it is quite common for students to transcribe improvised solos, note-for-note, from recordings. In addition to discovering what notes are played, students are encouraged to emulate every nuance that the artist employs. Short and long notes, scoops into notes, straight tone, vibrato—slow and fast—everything. In other words the student's goal is to temporarily become that musician on the recording. This requires very intense listening skills. It also requires repetition. The process helps the student assimilate the style of the player. The visual arts employ the same form of study. Art students copy from the masters as an acknowledged part of their education. At the Louvre, or any major art museum, it is not uncommon to see small groups of students working at their easels in front of the Mona Lisa, for example. It's a form of copying whose end goal is not to sound (or paint) exactly like the person being copied, but to internalize and build a stylistic vocabulary. By doing this over a period of time, and with recordings of many different jazz artists, the student will begin to find his or her own voice.

Knowing the competition is essential if you have an invention or an idea for a book, for example. One of the first things you should do is see what has already been published in that area. Do some research. My first book was called *Pentatonic Scales for Jazz Improvisations.* It was written in 1974 and first published in 1975 by a company called Studio PR. At that time there weren't nearly as many published improvisation books available as there are today. My book was different in that it described how to employ a certain harmonic concept to jazz improvisation—the pentatonic scale.

I began this enterprise, not with the idea of writing a book, but just trying to figure out, for myself, what the great players of the time, who used pentatonics as part of their harmonic vocabulary, were doing. I put my thoughts down on paper and then discovered that I might have a book here. So I did some research. I determined that a book like this would be unique, and that it would fill a gap in the jazz instructional literature. After it was written I started researching publishers. I made a list of those that published jazz books. I then went to the music store in town that carried the widest selection of sheet music. I simply asked the owner for his advice. What companies would be good for this book? From a dealer's standpoint, which one is the best to work with? He suggested that a small startup company, Studio PR, would be good and that just by chance their vice-president would be making a trip to Rochester in two weeks. I could meet him and show him what I had. The music store owner would set it up.

Two weeks passed. We met and I showed the VP one of my copies. The book was "camera ready," and I had made 30 copies for friends and colleagues. He could see that, with the exception of designing a cover, they would have relatively little to do to publish it. It was "roll the presses." The VP took it back, showed it to his boss and one week later it was accepted. Studio PR was bought by Columbia Pictures a few years later, and has changed hands several times in the intervening years. The book is currently published by Alfred and after all this time it still sells several hundred copies a year. This little story also reminds me that with all the books I have published I have always had a friend or associate who made an initial inquiry for me. I have never sent something "cold" to a publisher. Try to do the same if you are looking to publish.

Manage Your Time Well

To be a successful professional, somewhere along the way you must learn to manage your time effectively. I'm sure you have friends and acquaintances who have lots of projects going on and many responsibilities, but they always seem to get things done. They meet their deadlines, and with high quality as well. On the other hand there are some who are always behind—not responding to emails and coming up with excuse after excuse for missed deadlines—always "a day late and a dollar short." They may be equally talented or smart, but they don't seem to get 100 percent out of their innate ability. It could be a time management issue.

What I have done, and it works for me, is to be very aware of both my short-term and long-term commitments, and to continually monitor them. Periodically I'll look over my schedule for the next month or two. It reminds me of what is coming up and if there is something I need to start immediately attending to, I'll know it. "Oh, we're playing the Shostakovich Violin Concerto next month. I better start looking at that music right now. It's difficult and exposed." On a more near-term, weekly basis, I will probably take a few minutes on a Sunday night to look over my schedule for the coming week. I'll look for "white space" (read: free time) in it where I will have opportunities to prepare for the weekly events. If it is a light week, I'll do some work on that Shostakovich piece. When focusing on daily activities, I will check my next day's schedule each morning or at the end of the previous day. This helps me ensure that I don't overlook something that needs preparation, or that I need to think about.

Email! Sometimes it feels like that's what my job is. Answering email. In the days of memos and phone messages we had some slack built in. But today the current expectation for returning business messages seems to be at minimum by the end of the day. Here is what I do to handle email. For each business-related email I receive, I try to answer it as soon as I can. I do a quick answer—one or two sentences. If it will require me to spend more time than I can afford at the moment, I will send back a reply that says something like, "Got it. I'll reply in greater detail tomorrow, or later in the week." This gets them off my back. On emails where several people have been copied in, I will hold back and let the others chime in first. Often the issue gets resolved before I reply. Or sometimes one of these "first responders" will have the same point of view as me and exactly articulate my thoughts. In that case all I have to do is say, "I agree with Leslie." Still other times, to avoid extensive back and forth, I simply say, "Let's talk by phone."

My advice is to avoid lengthy emails. Short and to the point is best. Try to address only one issue. Emails on subjects that are complicated and multi-faceted could require several hours of thought and writing to answer. Save those discussions for one-on-one meetings.

Stick to a Schedule

From Rochester, New York to New York City it is about 350 miles, and it takes six hours to drive it by car. If I need to be in NYC at 6:00 P.M., I can't leave at 2:00 P.M. and expect to make it on time. Think of your busy life in the same manner. Think backward from due dates. Just this week a student came to me. She had a project due in a class that I teach—Entrepreneurship in Music. She wanted to turn in the assignment late because her flute teacher told her that she can't do anything but practice for her recital for the next week and a half. This tells me that this student has not been taking care of business! She left for NYC two or three hours late and if she does make it on time it will require speeding and lots of luck.

My schedule is set with lessons to give, a class to teach, meetings to attend, rehearsals and concerts to play and decisions to make. It can get filled up very quickly. But inherent in each of these obligations is preparation. I need to figure out how I will prepare for all of these events and how I am going to accomplish all that is required of me. I need a schedule for the "white space." I don't write out a schedule for myself, but I have one in my head. I calculate the amount of time that a particular task will take to complete. For example, if I have a letter of recommendation to write for a student for whom I've never written one before, it may take me 45 minutes. On the other hand, if I already have written a letter for her and it is in my file, all I have to do is tweak it. That might take just 10 minutes. In writing this book I created a schedule in my mind. It was fairly loose until I determined how fast or slow things would go. Knowing that things happen and it is easy to get sidetracked, I made it a rule that on each day that I had available to write, I would start the day working on the book. If I got 1,000 words, I would be happy and then I could relax or do something else.

Younger students often have a difficult time figuring out how to get things done. For my private one-on-one students who have this problem, I have asked them to write out a schedule for each day. Fill in the class time, then schedule study, homework and practice time. I have them bring it to their lesson for me to see. The reverse also works. I have had some students take one week, write down what they did in each hour of the day, and show it to me the following week. This can be quite telling and useful in showing students where they can be more efficient. Now, I'm not advocating working all the time. Free time and socializing is important too, but you'll have more occasions for that if you get your work done as quickly and efficiently as possible.

Getting Ahead

Make the Client Feel Good

This short phrase, "Make the client feel good," is one of the most important things to remember in business. Often when doing recording sessions for television and radio commercials (read: jingles) the "composer" may be a person of little of no musical knowledge. He may not even read music or be able to put one note down on the page for others to play. We call composers like this "hummers." The successful ones hire talented musicians to interpret what they are imagining in their heads, and during the composition process there are often non-musical instructions. Things like: "keep going up here," "it's too thin," "it's too confusing," "I want to feel like I'm in a convertible, driving down a country road and the wind is in my hair." Or this one that was going to be music behind a ski plane landing in the wilderness. "Don't use a saxophone! Saxophones are for cities!"

The fact is that these people, whether musically literate or not, got the gig. And, you know, they do have something to offer because this product will be seen and heard by the general public and not by concertgoers seated in a theatre audience. Rather than working against them, it is better to work with them and interpret their wishes as best as possible. The music for a cat food commercial isn't in the same league as a Mahler symphony, but if, in the end, it helps convey the intended message it has done its job. So I let them know it. I want to be extremely cooperative and "into" that commercial. I want them to know that, for that session, I was on their team, and trying my best to add value to the product.

In the above example it is easy to picture the client. But I also think of the word "client" more broadly. When I'm playing second clarinet in an orchestra, my client is the first clarinetist and the conductor. I want them to feel very good about my work. Is the tuning, balance and phrasing all good? If I were a rhythm section musician in jazz group, when not soloing, my job would be to comp (read: accompany and communicate musically with) the soloist. In my role as an administrator in a music school, my client is anyone above me or below me in the hierarchy. Attempting to please those above you is obvious. We all try to do that. But people below us in the organization chart often come to us to solve problems or ask advice. They can be our clients, too.

When those around us feel personally good about our work and us, we get asked back. And that's the name of the game—getting asked back. You will if you make the client feel good.

Know When To Take a Solo

No, I'm not talking about a musical solo. I'm talking about those moments that occur in meetings or discussions when you decide to make a comment. There are probably hundreds of different scenarios that can be imagined, but let's take just one to make the point. If I'm with my boss and we have been invited to a meeting (the purpose of the meeting doesn't matter) I let him "play lead." I "play second." If he's considerate he may pull me into the conversation by deferring to me or asking me to comment. That's when I solo! Even if I know more about the details of the subject under discussion, I don't lead off the conversation. He can frame it and provide the big picture. I can get down to more specifics. We all have a boss regardless of the status we may achieve within our professions. Knowing "how to play lead," "how to play second" and "when to take a solo" is important. When in doubt, play second.

Know the Rules

Every organization has its rules. In an orchestra many of these rules will be written in its contract between management and the musicians. But group cultures develop through custom, and many unwritten rules can take shape over time—an unspoken protocol results. If you are new to a job you must be sensitive to the nuances of the organization. For example, some orchestras have a reputation as being confrontational with management. In these orchestras it can be common for individuals to file grievances over perceived infractions of the union contract. If a musician comes from one of these more militant cultures to an orchestra that is more friendly and collegial toward management, he may be viewed as a troublemaker. If he doesn't pick up on this, he may have a difficult time operating in this environment. Leave the blinders at home. Have your antenna out. Get the feel of the group. Read the context of the situation.

There Is Always a System

Every organization has a system and a culture. In a music school it may be written down someplace in a faculty or student handbook, or in the case of an orchestra it may be outlined in the union bargaining agreement between the players and management. In a corporation it may be reflected in an organization chart, but these documents probably do not accurately reflect the manner in which the organization *really* works. A new person to any group has to recognize the centers of power. Within each department of a school or section of an orchestra there are leaders who may, or may not, always be the department chair or principal player. In contrast to the acknowledged, *formal* leaders, these people are the *informal* leaders in the group. These are people who are respected and may have the ear of the higher-ups. They are people who can get things done and make something happen. Identify these people and seek their advice. They have been down this road before, and they know where the potholes are. Learn the system.

Don't Change the System: Work through It–Then Change It

Once the system becomes clear to you, you may see things with which you don't agree, but don't waste a lot of time trying to change it. The headwind will be too strong. Play by the rules (read: culture) that are already in place. As you climb up the ladder and gain the respect of your colleagues, your day will come when you can exert your influence and make the organization better.

Go Cheap at the Outset

At the beginning of one's career it is important to be frugal. All things relating to your business should take precedent. You need the best instruments. You may also need a computer, music software, maybe a keyboard and a home studio setup. These are your tools and are an investment in You, Inc. (They are also tax deductible.) Budget wisely and live within your means. Take care of business first. It will pay off in the long run.

Improvise

Much of the information in this book emphasizes planning. Certainly it's important to have a plan and goals, to act rather than react, and to look for opportunities. But not everything always goes according to plan. In those instances don't just freeze up. Improvise. If you don't have time to think it through, go with your gut feelings. Sometimes you do have to "wing it." Nine times out of ten, you'll make the right choice. I often say, and I wish I knew where I read it, that with many projects it is necessary to build the bridge as we walk on it.

Trust, Loyalty and Commitment

These are all personality or character traits that we, as humans, like to see in our friends and business associates. Most of us will weed out, or won't allow people to get close to us who appear disloyal or untrustworthy. We may still relate to them on some level, but we will keep them at arm's length. Your superiors, peers and subordinates alike, as well as your clients, need to know that you are a straight shooter and that you are committed to them. But this is not something that is gained by you telling them how loyal you are. They learn this over time by your actions, and make no mistake—they'll be watching.

Attention to Detail and Immediate Follow-Up

Everyone with whom you interact, whether it is on a personal or business level, appreciates a person who "takes care of business." If I am asked to put a large group together to play, let's say an opera, I'll move this request to the top of my list and I'll have a price for them by the next day. If it is a smaller group I try to have it to them by the end of the day. Invariably they will thank me for being so prompt. They have received the message that I "take care of business." I will also go over their requirements looking for ways to save them money. This is particularly important when booking lots of musicians for several services—like an opera. The bill will be high and any cost-cutting suggestions are always appreciated. These little things give the client (contractor or leader) confidence that they have called the right person and that you know what you are doing.

Don't Use a Gig to Make a Personal Statement

Jazz and commercial musicians still get calls today to play big band gigs where the music will be from the 1940s and '50s. This music should be played in the style of the period, and that goes for improvised solos as well. Just think World War II, Glen Miller, Benny Goodman and Harry James. A less adventurous harmonic vocabulary is used and there is a heavy triplet feel in the eighth-note lines. It's old and dated sounding. When a person takes one of these jobs he should know what he is getting into. It's fun music to play, but you won't be breaking any new ground that night.

I can recall one occasion when I put one of these bands together for a musician from out of town. He brought the music and the stands. His name was nationally known, but the musicians were all local and they sight-read the job. (This is actually fairly common.) It was a good gig. The band sounded fine, but toward the end of the evening one of the saxophonists decided he was going to show everyone in the band what he knew. He had to improvise a solo over a simple, sort of "bluesy" chord progression. He should have been riffing away in the harmonic vocabulary of the period, but to use musician's vernacular, he "took it out." It wasn't appropriate and it didn't fit. In effect he was saying, "I'm cool. Look at me. I don't have to play by these rules." He was making a personal statement. Nobody bought it.

Never Go One-on-One with the Boss

I should add another phrase to this. "Never go one-on-one with the boss, because even when you think you win—you lose." Most bosses appreciate it when their subordinates speak with them in an honest and straightforward manner. But there is a line that cannot be crossed without doing permanent damage to your relationship. I'm speaking about those conversations that escalate and approach the, "I'm going to win at any cost" level. Go ahead, deliver your information and your opinion, but you must know when to pull back. Your boss is your boss.

I've witnessed these contests from time to time with music school faculty and administrators. When a faculty member is tenured there are only a handful of situations (and they must be egregious) that can cause a person to lose his job. Because of this, certain personality types can feel emboldened to speak their mind. Taking on the boss, especially in a public forum, is tantamount to job suicide. You may think you have won, but believe me, the incident is tucked away in the back of your superior's head, and somewhere down the road you will pay for it. Opportunities may come across his desk that may be a good fit for you, but if you have burned him, you won't be on his, "I want to help this guy" list. And the ironic thing is that most likely you won't even be aware that you have missed out on something. It's human nature that we reward our supporters and try to neutralize our detractors. Be a supporter. Your boss is your boss.

P.S.: If you are a freelancer, you have a different boss at every engagement. For every reference to "your boss" in this section, just substitute contractor, leader, producer, promoter, audience, donor, supporter and client.

What an Internship Can Teach You

Interns don't run companies. Most supervisors try very hard to give them interesting assignments that will be learning opportunities, but the nature of their job is such that from time to time there will be some mundane assignments that come their way. It's how a person handles these uninteresting tasks that gives me clues about their potential for excelling when school is out. Many high achievers seem to have a need to do well no matter what they are asked to do. Take a boring job like stuffing envelopes—they will set up a system and get a rhythm going. As they move toward completion they will monitor their progress—"Just passed 25 percent completions." They seem to recognize that the job has to be done, and they might as well do it as well as possible. These personality types are achievers with good attitudes, and they carry that trait throughout their lives. Believe me, even people higher up in the food chain occasionally have duties to perform that are less than glamorous.

Negotiation

Life is filled with occasions when we must negotiate. We buy a house or a car (that's a distasteful one). Someone hires us to put together a group to play for a wedding reception or a bar mitzvah. We might do an arrangement of music for a marching band half-time show, jazz ensemble or a community orchestra. All the details need to be discussed and agreed to—details like: date and time, number of musicians and instrumentation. If it is an arranging or composition project you must agree on the number of minutes of music, instrumentation and the date when the music will be delivered. And in all these instances it is always necessary to discuss money. These negotiations rarely become contentious. After all, they have contacted you and are already close to hiring you. But symphony musicians may be elected by their orchestra's rank and file to serve on the contract negotiation committee. That can be a more lengthy process, and it has the potential of getting ugly. Negotiation is arriving at a middle ground. They want something. You want something. Somehow, in the end, both parties must feel good about the outcome. Here are some things to remember.

Have Your Price in Mind

You should have a price in mind for the particular service that is under discussion. Different types of gigs will have different pay rates that are either set by the musicians' union or are the going rates of the area. Many jobs pay scale and that's it. A traveling Broadway show or an opera put on by the local company are examples. Union scale is the minimum amount that a union musician can be paid for a particular job, but there is no limit to the amount that can be paid over scale. When figuring the budget I usually start with union scale, then factor in costs for other things like travel, cartage of large instruments and percussion rental. If you have a string quartet, for example, and someone wants to hire you for a wedding reception, it won't be so complicated. You'll have a price, and there will be little back and forth discussion.

But money isn't the only consideration. I have taken lots of work that didn't pay well, on the hope that it would lead to something bigger down the road. Sometimes it does and sometimes it doesn't.

Let the Other Guy Talk First

Writing projects (read: compositions and arrangements) are always up for negotiation. What I always try to do is let the person hiring me talk first. After we have discussed what is involved, I quickly calculate how much time it will take to complete it. I get a price in my head that I think is fair, but I try to let the other person make an offer. If he doesn't come forward with a figure, and assuming I know the person pretty well, I might say something like this. "What's your budget for this? Have you got any money?" He'll probably come back with something like, "I think I can get $2,000." Many, many times that figure will be more than I was thinking. Now, if I don't know the person I won't be so flip in getting him to talk. I'll say, "What have you budgeted for this project?" I have found that often what seems like a lot of money to a musician is not that much to the person who is hiring you.

It can work the other way too. A good friend contacted me about one of my unpublished big-band charts. "Can you get me a copy?" he asked. "Sure, how about $75 delivered?" I replied. Pausing, he said, "Look, I'll give you $150." That's a good friend. I was trying to do him a favor, but he had the money in his budget, and he took care of me. (The $150 was a fair price.)

"I see your point, but . . ."

Negotiating fees for music for a wedding or figuring budgets based on union scale do not require extensive negotiating skills. It is what it is, more or less. However, if you have to negotiate an orchestra contract, or the terms of a new job that you have been offered, it can get dicey. It's important that you recognize the other side's point of view and understand it. But that doesn't mean that you must agree with it. I've been known to say something like, "I understand why you are proposing that, but look at it from our point of view. This just won't work for us. We have . . ."

Do It in Person

You can take care of many things via email, but in negotiation discussions I prefer to talk face to face. Absent that, the telephone is an okay second choice for me. In direct conversations you read body language. If you have said something that has not been taken well, you can soften it as you continue to speak. With email it's possible to come off much harsher than you really are. If being understood is important to you, do it in person.

Be Prepared

"Be Prepared" is the Boy Scout's motto, but it also applies to negotiations. The week, day or night before you are to meet, you should think through some different possible scenarios. First of all, anticipate the major points that may be presented by the other party and formulate some responses. Prioritize them. Not all will be a big deal to you. Secondly, play through a possible conversation in your head, talking aloud or even writing your thoughts down. It could be something like the following. You fill in the blanks. "I'm going to say ____. If he replies with ____, then I'm going to say ____. If he doesn't go there, and instead says ____, then I'll say ____." And so on. There's a reason the boy scouts' motto is "Be Prepared." Everything goes better that way.

Separate Personalities from the Issues

Negotiating should not be about winning. It should be about getting to a place that is mutually satisfactory for both parties. Occasionally you may be up against a person whose personality just grates on you. You may not like him or her, and his or her "style" might be very adversarial and confrontational, but you have to put it aside. Be cool. If you let your emotions run, you can start fixating on one-upmanship and "winning." Don't take your eye off the prize—getting an agreement.

Avoid Showdowns

If you fail to separate the issues from personalities the result can turn into a showdown. Egos and machismo can come into play. What starts out as a contract negotiation can turn into, "I'll show that guy. He can't do that to me." When it gets to this point, it's probably strike or lock out time, and that's not good. Avoid "drawing a line in the sand" and announcements of "dealbreakers." Don't be drawn into a contest.

It Ain't Over Till It's Over

When you have successfully gone through the interview process, come out on top and received a verbal offer, it's easy to think that you have got the job. But you haven't. Details still have to be negotiated—like your salary! Up until this point the money issue has probably not been fully addressed. If you are coming from another position, your potential new employer is aware of your present salary, and from your side you have a ballpark idea of what similar jobs pay. They want you; you want them. So what could go wrong? Just remember the words of Yogi Berra, "It ain't over till it's over."

A position became available in my office at Eastman. It was entry-level and we had more than 60 applicants for it, but one clearly stood out. He was young, energetic and had done well as an intern in a similar position at another school. His interview was wonderful. He hit every question thrown at him right out of the ballpark. As we did our due diligence some negatives began to surface, but they were several years in the past when this person was young. He has grown up, we thought (or rationalized), and besides he had done so well in the interview. He had some blemishes, but we would take a chance. He was our man.

I put in a call and gave him the good news. I told him that we would hammer out the details, and when we were both in agreement a written offer would be given. We set up a meeting for the following day. During the phone conversation he asked me the salary and I told him it was $36,500. This was an offer pre-determined by Human Resources and was based on job responsibilities, experience and comparable salaries for similar jobs within the university. He was disappointed that it wasn't more, but I said we would talk tomorrow.

At our meeting he came prepared with national salary averages for the position, and information on current openings in the area. He made his case and I told him that I would contact Human Resources to see if the salary could be bumped. Both of us noted that the salaries for similar jobs in the area were higher, but I reminded him that we weren't really comparing apples to apples with his figures. Some positions called for more experienced persons with more responsibility. I reminded him that this was his first real job and though internships are helpful in gaining job know-how they aren't like the real thing. We talked about the job's benefits, like health insurance and the two courses per semester that he could take free of charge. He could get another degree if he wanted. But within the positives I also brought up some of the negatives we had heard when checking references. I wanted him to know we had some reservations, but were willing to take a chance. He left the meeting with my pledge that I would try to get the salary higher.

Later that day, HR called with the news that another $1,000 had been secured, bringing the total to $37,500. I called our candidate. He was not happy, but I stated that I didn't think any more money was possible for this position. He said he would be out of town the next day, but would get back to me with an answer on the day after tomorrow. That day came and around 9:00 A.M. he called and asked if we could meet. I said we could meet at noon for half an hour, but added that the discussion of salary was off the table—$37,500 is the final offer. At that point he reiterated that he viewed the job as a $40K job and he wanted to discuss the job responsibilities. I told him that he had the job description. It became apparent to me that our noon meeting would include an attempt by him to reduce his duties to what he considered a $37,500 job. As this conversation unfolded I recognized that there was a strong potential that we might be about to hire an already disgruntled employee. The negatives that had surfaced from others were coming to the fore for me. I detected a slight tone of "attitude" in his voice. I lost all confidence in him and realized that he was not a good fit with us. I got off the phone with him and immediately contacted our HR representative to see if the job offer could be taken back. He indicated that it could. At 10:30 I called our candidate and rescinded the verbal offer. I could tell in his voice that he was crest-fallen. He really wanted the job and had no other prospects. He probably didn't think that taking the offer off the table could be possible, but it was.

As one negotiates a contract, especially if you are coming to a new position, you must remember that you are still being interviewed and evaluated. At all times remain cordial. Don't let a "tone" sneak into your voice. It's okay to push back, but you have to read the other guy. If you truly want the job, but are just trying to get a higher salary, be careful and don't push too hard. To me it's much better to accept the job. Your foot is in the door, now work your tail off. The raises will come, and if they don't, you'll have experience to move on to something else that pays more.

What Contractors Like

Someone Who Is Available

Contractors and leaders make lots of phone calls and send lots of emails. Consequently, they want to avoid dead end calls. They want to get the gig booked as quickly as possible, and so if individuals continually turn them down, they will eventually be passed over. It's not that they don't want to hire them, they just want to avoid making a call that has a high probability of going nowhere. If you want to stay on a contractor's list, do everything you can to make yourself available when he or she calls.

Someone Who Is Loyal (They Will Be Loyal in Return)

In the freelance world, loyal people are those who value the work that a contractor offers and do everything possible to make themselves available. Not every gig a contractor gets will be good. Good gigs: pay well, don't suck up a lot of your time, are with musicians you respect and enjoy being around, involve music that you like to play, and have possibilities for repeat work. Bad gigs: don't pay well, often involve travel by car, could involve working with a boorish leader and usually involve music you aren't crazy about playing. But sometimes you have to say yes to one of these "bad gigs" just to stay in the good graces of the contractor. That's loyalty. They remember when a musician does them a favor. If you are loyal to them, they will be sure to reciprocate by passing "good work" your way the next time around.

Someone Who Is Always on Time (If You're on Time, You're Late)

Being punctual is very important in the music business. If a rehearsal has to start late because of a musician, it can open the door for difficult money talks at the end of the gig or session. Often the person hiring you will say, and rightly so, "You started 15 minutes late. We need to adjust your fee." Or if it is a recording session and it has to go into overtime, the producer will not want to pay the extra amount that was caused by a late musician.

It is common practice for orchestras to levy fines on tardy musicians, and the amount for each infraction is written into the master agreement. Late to a rehearsal, late to a concert, and late back from intermission all have different degrees of severity assigned to them. Late to a concert will be a higher fine than late to a rehearsal. Think about it. You can't be looking around for the first trumpet player when the concert is ready to begin. The master agreement will also more than likely stipulate that the musicians must be in their seats five minutes prior to the start of the service. As a group, orchestra musicians are very time conscious. And this part of the orchestra culture bleeds over into their everyday life. If you are throwing a party and it starts at 7:00 P.M., the orchestra folks will be there at 7:00 P.M. There will be none of this fashionably late business.

When I book a large number of musicians for an out of town concert, and they have all driven there separately, there is always that moment of truth. As we assemble on stage for the rehearsal, I look around hoping that everyone has made it on time and that they will be there for the start. I always breathe a sigh of relief when I see that everyone has arrived. The most important part of the gig is over. We're all here! The music will take care of itself.

Someone Who Makes Them Look Good

There is a great feeling when a producer, conductor or the person who has hired you asks, "Who's the new guy on trumpet? He sounds great!"

Contractors are responsible (read: their ass is on the line) for the quality of the music that the musicians produce. If a particular person is having trouble with a passage and the conductor is giving them a hard time, we feel it too. It only happened to me once, and it was many years ago, but a conductor of a national touring company of a Broadway show asked me to fire the bass player and replace him. He was just not cutting the part. He was a fine jazz bassist, and I was giving him a shot at this very good paying "reading gig," but he wasn't up to it. My mistake. When the players sound good, the contractor looks good, and that translates into repeat work.

Someone Who Doesn't Ask Dumb Questions

I remember teachers saying, "There are no dumb questions." Well, not so in real life! There are a couple types of dumb questions that are asked frequently in music. The first type is the question that is asked just to make the person asking it look smart. "At letter D do I have an f-natural or an f-sharp? It's f-sharp in my part." (Everyone else in the group has an f-natural. We all heard it was supposed to be an f-natural. Why are we wasting time on this!)

The second type is the inappropriately timed question. It's a large group and you are assembling on stage for a rehearsal that afternoon and a concert that evening. There is always a certain amount of confusion in these situations. No one knows where they are supposed to sit. There is hammering going on as the set gets put into place. A carload of musicians hasn't arrived yet and the start time is approaching. In short—your pants are on fire. The insensitive musician may ask, "Will they have food for us?" Save this type of question for after the rehearsal, when all fires have been put out and the music has been rehearsed.

CHAPTER 11

Coda

Now we come to the end of these "lessons from a street-wise professor," and this short coda should serve to tie it all up and put a bow on it. But how should I do that? What are the most important lessons to be taken from this book? As I look at the table of contents it reminds me that there is a story here.

I don't exactly know what Cliff Notes or Graphic Novels are because they came on the scene after I was out of high school. But I am familiar with Classic Comics. In my day they were the comic book version of important literary works, and for a high school book report they came in very handy. It strikes me that this might be a good spot for a condensed, Classic Comics version (without the illustrations) of my lessons. So, here we go.

- It's tough out there in the real world of professional music.

- But, with your Legos you can build your career—You, Inc.
  - You, Inc. will be unique and shaped around your strengths, talents and interests.

- Your goal is to separate yourself from the pack and be noticed.

- It's also your goal to stay relevant, engaged in what you do, and to put a career together that provides a comfortable living.
  - That requires more than just fantastic performing skills and superb musicianship.
  - That's where entrepreneurial thinking comes in.
    - Adding entrepreneurial savvy to your already sound playing and artistry will give you a competitive advantage.

- Take charge of your career. Be pro-active. Make something happen.

- Build your brand

- BUT—be ready for a non-linear career path
  - Doors will open and doors will close—be ready for both.
  - Recognize and take advantage of opportunities.

- Ask yourself why you play music. What is your *raison d'être*?

- Make a plan. You're at point A. You want to be at point B. What are the necessary steps you must take to get there?

- Set some goals, and don't be timid about it.

- Get some business chops. Learn the nitty-gritty of the music business.
  - Taxes, lawyers, recordings, getting gigs, grant money, dealing with people, the web, royalties, etc.
  - Learn how to preserve and grow your wealth.

- Recognize that everyone's career journey will be different, but some recurring lessons that successful musicians have learned seem to be these:
  - Be the best at what you do.
  - Look for and recognize opportunities.
  - Don't be afraid to do something that hasn't been done before.
  - Keep your art at a high level. Don't dilute it.
  - Don't be afraid to take calculated risks.
  - Don't give up on yourself.
  - Work toward a goal.

- Look at the table of contents of this book, especially Chapter 10. What do you think are the most important lessons to remember for professional musicians? Here's my list, along with some backup from some important thinkers. See if you agree.

Make a pledge to quality.

"When you're out of quality, you're out of business." — unknown author

Make the client feel good.

"They may forget what you said, but they will never forget how you made them feel." — Carl W. Buehner (1898–1974), former leader in The Church of Jesus Christ of Latter-day Saints

Be a life-long learner.

"Learning is not a product of schooling but the lifelong attempt to acquire it." — Albert Einstein (1879–1955), physicist and Nobel Laureate

Have a career not a job.

"The difference between a job and a career is the difference between forty and sixty hours a week." — Robert Frost (1874–1963), American poet

Always remember why you decided on a career in music.

"A bird doesn't sing because it has an answer, it sings because it has a song." — Maya Angelou (1928–), American author and poet

Keep your dream alive.

"Twenty years from now you will be more disappointed by the things that you didn't do than by the ones you did do. So throw off the bowlines. Sail away from the safe harbor. Catch the trade winds in your sails. Explore. Dream. Discover." — Mark Twain (1835–1910), pen name of Samuel Langhorne Clemens, American author and humorist

BIBLIOGRAPHY

Beeching, Angela Myles. *Beyond Talent—Creating a Successful Career in Music.* New York: Oxford University Press, 2005.

Blum, Laurie. *The Complete Guide to Getting a Grant.* New York: John Wiley & Son, Inc., 1996.

Bornstein, David. *How to Change the World.* New York: Oxford University Press, 2007.

Cohn, Al and Bob Kohn. *The Art of Music Licensing.* New York: Prentice Hall Law and Business, 1992.

Collins, Jim. *Good to Great.* New York: Harper Collins, 2001.

Drucker, Peter F. *Innovation and Entrepreneurship.* New York: Harper Business, 1993.

Gerber, Michael E. *The E Myth Revisited.* Harper Business, 1995.

Grant, Daniel. *The Business of Being an Artist.* New York: Allworth Press, 2000.

Heflick, David. *How to Make Money Performing in Schools.* Orient, WA: Silcox Productions, 1996.

Highstein, Ellen. *Making Music in Looking Glass Land.* New York: Concert Artists Guild, 2003.

Hupalo, Peter I. *Thinking Like an Entrepreneur.* St. Paul, MN: HCM Publishing, 2004.

Knopper, Steve. *Appetite for Self-Destruction (The Spectacular Crash of the Record Industry in the Digital Age).* New York: Free Press, 2009.

Krasilovsky, M. William and Sydney Shemel with contributions by John M. Gross and Jonathan Feinstein. *This Business of Music.* New York: Watson-Guptill Publications, 2007.

Liberatori, Ellen. *Guide to Getting Arts Grants.* New York: Allworth Press, 2006.

Manduca, Elizabeth M. and Alison Barr. *A Practical Guide to Successful Studio Teaching.* Portland, ME: The Piano Teacher's Press, 1993.

McCormack, Mark H. *What They Don't Teach You at Harvard Business School.* New York: Bantom Books, 1984.

McGrath, Rita Gunther and Ian MacMillan. *The Entrepreneurial Mindset.* Boston: Harvard Business School Press, 2000.

Newsam, David R. and Barbara Sprague Newsam. *Making Money Teaching Music.* Cincinnati, OH: Writer's Digest Books, 1995.

Passman, Donald. *All You Need to Know about the MUSIC BUSINESS.* New York: Simon and Schuster, 1991.

Quinn, Robert E. *Deep Change.* San Francisco: Jossey-Bass, 1996.

Schramm, Carl J. *The Entrepreneurial Imperative.* New York: Harper Collins, 2006.

Spellman, Peter. *The Musician's Internet.* Boston: Berklee Press, 2002.

Steinberg, Irwin and Harmon Greenblatt. *Understanding the Music Business.* Needham Heights, MA: Simon and Schuster Custom Publishing, 1998.

Thall, Peter M. *What They'll Never Tell You about the Music Business.* New York: Watson-Guptill Publications, 2002.

Uscher, Nancy. *Your Own Way in Music.* New York: St. Martin's Press, 1990.

ENDNOTES

1. *Facts and Figures Concerning Music and Higher Education in the United States,* The College Music Society. Revised November 2009. http://www.music.org/pdf/outreach/FactsandFigures.pdf.

2. *Music Data Summaries, 2009–2010,* Higher Education Arts Data Services, National Association of Schools of Music. http://nasm.arts-accredit.org/index.jsp?page=Statistical%20Information.

3. *Facts and Figures Concerning Music and Higher Education in the United States,* The College Music Society. Revised November 2009. http://www.music.org/pdf/outreach/FactsandFigures.pdf.

4. Joseph Nocera, "Chicken Hawker," *New York Times,* Dec. 25, 2005.

5. The International Conference of Symphonic and Opera Musicians (ICSOM) represents more than 4,000 musicians in the top 51 American Federation of Musicians orchestras in the United States and Puerto Rico.

6. Daniel J. Wakin, "Four Major Orchestras Facing Contract Issues," *The New York Times,* Sept. 16, 2004.

7. William Cahn, personal correspondence via email, August 10, 2008.

8. For those of you too young to remember, Deputy Dawg was a cartoon character from the '60s whose personality was less than upbeat.

9. *The American Heritage Dictionary of the English Language:* Fourth Edition. 2000.

10. David A. Aaker and Erich Joachimsthaler, *Brand Leadership* (New York: The Free Press, 2000), p. 17.

11. Marianne Foley, *In-Market Validation of Connections-Based Research,* Harris Interactive, Inc. (executive brief) 2007.

[12] Kevin Lane Keller, *Strategic Brand Management* (Upper Saddle River, NJ: Prentice Hall, 1998), p. 5.

[13] ibid.

[14] Aaker and Joachimsthaler, *Brand Leadership*, p. 40–41.

[15] Shelly Banjo and Kelly K. Spors, "Musician Finds a Following Online," *The Wall Street Journal*, Small Business—Enterprise section, Dec. 30, 2008.

[16] Ellen Liberatori, *Guide to Getting Arts Grants* (New York: Allworth Press, 2006), p. 7.

[17] Harry Fox website. http://www.harryfox.com.

[18] Bernard Korman and I. Fred Koenigsberg, "Performing Rights in Music and Performing Right Societies," *Journal of the Copyright Society of the USA*, Vol. 33, No.4 (July 1986), p. 348.

[19] Signature Sound Website, "Eleven Most Frequently Asked Questions About Music Licensing," http://www.signature-sound.com/11quest.html#q3.

[20] "What Are Patents, Trademarks, Servicemarks, and Copyrights?", United States Patent and Trademark Office website. http://www.uspto.gov/web/offices/pac/doc/general/whatis.htm.

[21] William T. Hunt, "Depreciation of Musical Instruments," polyphonic.org, April 10, 2006. http://www.polyphonic.org/article.php?id=30&page=1.

[22] William T. Hunt, "Musicians and Home Office Tax Deductions," polyphonic .org, April 2, 2007. http://www.polyphonic.org/article.php?id=115&page=1.

[23] http://www.investorwords.com/4626/sole_proprietorship.html.

[24] http://www.investorwords.com/3609/partnership.html.

[25] http://www.investorwords.com/796/C_Corporation.html.

[26] http://www.investorwords.com/4411/S_Corporation.html.

[27] http://www.investorwords.com/2853/LLC.html.

[28] http://www.investorwords.com/5637/LLP.html.

[29] http://www.investorwords.com/3353/not_for_profit_organization.html.

[30] John C. Bogle, *Common Sense on Mutual Funds* (Hoboken, NJ: John C. Wiley and Sons, 2000), p 7.

[31] http://www.businessdictionary.com/definition/non-qualified-deferred-compensation-NQDC.html.

[32] http://treasurydirect.gov/indiv/products/products.htm.

[33] Nellie Mae is a subsidiary of the SLM Corporation, also known as Sally Mae, and in their words is "the nation's leading provider of student loans and

administrator of college savings plans." It was originally created in 1972 as a government-sponsored entity, but was privatized in 2004. SLM Corporation and its subsidiaries are not sponsored by or agencies of the U.S. Government.

[34] Erica Williams, "Students Need Help Combating Credit Card Debt: Testimony before the House Financial Services Subcommittee on Financial Institutions and Consumer Credit," Center for American Progress, June 26, 2008. http://www.americanprogress.org/issues/2008/06/williams_testimony.html.

[35] ibid.

[36] Mindy Fetterman and Barbara Hansen, "Young People Struggle to Deal with the Kiss of Debt," *USA Today,* Nov. 22, 2006. http://www.usatoday.com/money/perfi/credit/2006-11-19-young-and-in-debt-cover_x.htm.

[37] Recorded conversation with Maria Schneider on February 2, 2009.

[38] Ossia still exists today at the Eastman School and functions in the same manner as its founders established in 1996.

[39] http://www.alarmwillsound.com/events/current.html.

[40] Mark H. McCormack, *What They Don't Teach You At Harvard Business School* (New York: Bantam Books, 1984).

[41] When a musician plays more than one instrument on an engagement, they have what is called a "double," and they are paid a certain additional percentage, per instrument, to do this. For example, in show work it is quite common for the woodwind players to play several instruments. The first reed book may call for alto saxophone, soprano saxophone, clarinet, flute and piccolo. In this case the musician playing this "book" would have four additional instruments, or four doubles.

[42] http://www.diffen.com/difference/Career_vs_Job.

[43] http://www.polyphonic.org/article.php?id=97&show=all.

[44] A signatory is a signer of a document such as a treaty, contract or agreement. By signing you agree to follow the rules set forth in the document. Union musicians, who do recordings, are represented by the American Federation of Musicians (the musicians union—AFM), and within the AFM there is the Electronic Media Services Division (EMSD). It administers recording contracts that are negotiated between the AFM and record or production companies. There are many different agreements in place that deal with a wide variety of recording situations. Some of these agreements cover: sound recordings, industrial films, theatrical motion picture, television film, basic cable television, commercial announcements and National Public Radio.

[45] http://www.drakeceramicinstruments.com/.

APPENDIX A-INDEX OF LESSONS

Brand

Business

Business Entities

Career

Goals
Have goals. · 156
Keep your dream alive. · 179, 225
Keep your eye on the prize. · 134
Prepare yourself to follow your dream. · 21
Work toward a goal. · 134, 156, 224

Grants
Follow the grant application guidelines and rules to the letter. · 77
Once your application materials are assembled, apply for more than
    one grant. · 76
One thing leads to another. · 170

Ideas
An idea is just an idea until it is written down. · 45, 49, 170
An idea is just an idea until you act on it. · 149
Have an idea/project file. · 170

Insurance
Explore all available options for health insurance before going
    without. · 126

Law
Be careful when asked to sign any contract. You must understand
    it. · 62
Don't "do it yourself" when it comes to legal issues. Lawyers are your
    friends. · 99
Lawyers are paid for their time. Be prepared and get to the
    point. · 100

Money
Don't be embarrassed about making money. · 134, 180
Don't make money the number one objective—learn to wait. · 179
Don't talk money in front of others. · 171
Don't use credit cards to borrow money. · 123
Save money every month. · 110
Go cheap at the outset. · 156, 210

Music

Try not to be noticed. · 160

Versatility creates options. The more things you can do well the greater your options. · 37

Write down what you know. · 169

You don't have to be perfect all the time. · 175

You don't have to live in a large metropolitan area to have a fulfilling life in music. · 139

Your challenge is to break from the pack and be noticed. · 7, 13

Negotiation

Avoid showdowns. · 216

Drive a soft bargain. · 194

"I see your point, but..." · 215

It ain't over till it's over · 217

Let people off the hook. · 193

Let the other guy talk first. · 214

Separate personalities from the issues. · 216

Networking

Get your name around. · 63, 67, 101

Keep your network active and expanding. · 35

Make friends and acquaintances. · 139

Make friends—your peers are your best resource. · 159

Take advantage of personal connections to make business connections. · 150

Take every opportunity to play in master classes. Get noticed. · 34, 179

You may not know it now, but many of the people you meet in school will be working with you for the rest of your career. Keep the networks going. · 156

Quality

Be the best at what you do. · 2, 134, 139, 145, 150, 156, 160

Commit to quality. Add more product lines, but expand slowly. Don't dilute your core business. · 3, 18

Don't dilute your product in order to make money. · 3, 134, 156, 180, 224

Success

Success in music requires more than just fantastic technique and artistry. · xiv, 180

Success is being asked back. · 31

Think of "success" in small units. Celebrate your day-to-day successes. · 4

Taxes

An office in home will help with your taxes, but make sure it qualifies. · 96

Check your 1099s for accuracy. Errors tend to occur here with greater frequency than with W-2s. · 42

Even if you are paid in cash, you are still responsible to pay the IRS its due. · 102

Separate your business and personal finances, and keep good records. · 98, 102

Where taxes are concerned, if it seems too good to be true, it probably is. · 93

INDEX

ACKNOWLEDGEMENTS

I AM FORTUNATE TO HAVE very talented people around me who make me look good. That is certainly the case with this book. Thanks to Leslie Scatterday, who, in a conversation a little over a year ago said, "You should write a book." It's your fault, Leslie. I sincerely appreciate my friends and family who gave part of their valuable time to read and to offer encouragement and suggestions—Cheryl Stanton, Linda Altpeter, Chris Privett, Leah Ricker, Chien-Kwan Lin, Greg Sandow, Jim Doser, David Angus, Jamal Rossi and Jeff Tyzik. Special thanks are in order to Bill Hunt who checked and offered suggestions on the section on taxes, and to 1106 Design for their contribution to the look and feel of the book. My sister, Linda Ayres, is the brains in the Ricker family and her eagle eye, command of the English language and professional editing skills were put to good use here. Thank you, Linda. You're the best. And, of course, I must acknowledge my wife, Judy, who has always been my muse, prompting me and giving me inspiration, support and innumerable ideas for over three decades. And lastly to the three Eastman Deans for whom I have worked—Robert Freeman, for supporting, investing and having faith in me in my early years at Eastman, James Undercofler for entrusting me to make some of his pet projects happen, and Douglas Lowry for giving me the freedom to "drive the bus."

ABOUT THE AUTHOR

RAMON RICKER is Senior Associate Dean for Professional Studies, Director of the Institute for Music Leadership and Professor of Saxophone at the Eastman School of Music in Rochester, New York. As a senior administrator at Eastman, Dr. Ricker has been instrumental in shaping Eastman's innovative Arts Leadership curriculum that offers courses on Entrepreneurship and Careers, Leadership and Administration, Performance, Contemporary Orchestral Issues and The Healthy Musician. A full-time Eastman faculty member since 1972, he was the first titled saxophone professor at the school. He is also Editor-in-Chief of Polyphonic.org, an Eastman-sponsored website for professional orchestra musicians. From 1989 to 1998, he served as Chair of the Department of Winds, Brass and Percussion, and from 2000 to 2001 chaired Jazz Studies and Contemporary Media, co-chairing the same from 2001 to 2002.

His association with the Rochester Philharmonic Orchestra first began as a clarinet soloist in 1972. In 1974 he won a position in the RPO as a member of the clarinet section, and continues to play in the orchestra today. He served on its Board of Directors from 1997 to 2005.

He frequently performs as a guest saxophone and clarinet soloist and clinician in high schools and colleges throughout Europe and North America, and his books on jazz improvisation and saxophone technique as well as many of his compositions are looked to as standards in the field, with more than 140,000 copies sold worldwide with translations in French and Japanese.

He has performed and contracted the music for hundreds of television and radio commercials and themes, including national accounts for ABC, NBC, HBO and Arts and Entertainment. As a composer and arranger, he has been honored by grants from the National Endowment for the Arts, New York State Council on the Arts, Creative Artist Public Service, Meet the Composer and ASCAP. His arrangements have been commissioned by the Rochester Philharmonic and the American, Atlanta, Cincinnati and North Carolina Symphonies, with works published by Advance Music (Germany), Alphonse Leduc (Paris), ATN (Tokyo), Alfred (USA) and Jamey Aebersold (USA).

CPSIA information can be obtained at www.ICGtesting.com
Printed in the USA
268961BV00002B/15/P